Dr Eliot Attridge • Nathan Goodman • Dr Dorothy War

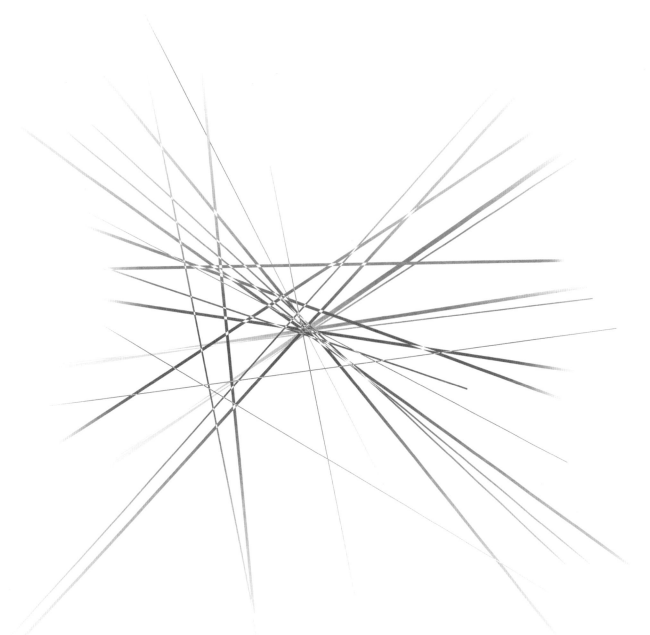

ESSENTIALS

OCR Twenty First Century
GCSE Science
Revision Guide

Contents

Contents

Acknowledgements

Acknowledgements

The authors and publisher would like to thank everyone who contributed images to this book:

p.8   ©iStockphoto.com / Linda Bucklin
p.12   ©iStockphoto.com / Patrick Hermans
p.25   ©iStockphoto.com / Luis Carlos Torres
p.25   ©iStockphoto.com / Aleksandr Volodin
p.25   ©iStockphoto.com / Kathy Hicks
p.35   ©iStockphoto.com / Nasa
p.37   ©iStockphoto.com / Steve O'Connor
p.37   ©iStockphoto.com / Christian Darkin
p.44   ©iStockphoto.com
p.46   ©iStockphoto.com / Peter Galbraith
p.59   ©iStockphoto.com / Tim Dalek
p.68   ©iStockphoto.com / Will Evans
p.75   ©iStockphoto.com / Linda Bucklin
p.95   ©iStockphoto.com

Data on p.23 provided by Pfizer.
Data on p.57 provided by Disposable Nappies: a case study in waste prevention, ©Women's Environmental Network, April 2003, www.wen.org.uk

ISBN 978-1-905896-41-7

Published by Lonsdale, a division of Huveaux PLC

Authors: Dr Eliot Attridge
Nathan Goodman
Dr Dorothy Warren
Steve Langfield

Project Editor: Robert Dean

Cover Design: Angela English

Concept design: Sarah Duxbury and Helen Jacobs

Designer: Joanne Hatfield

Artwork: Lonsdale

Lonsdale makes every effort to ensure that all paper used in its books is made from wood pulp obtained from well-managed forests, controlled sources and recycled wood or fibre.

Author Information

Dr Eliot Attridge (Biology) is a full member of the Institute of Biology, a chartered biologist (CBiol), and an experienced Head of Science. He works closely with the exam board as an Assistant Examiner for OCR Twenty First Century Science and was involved in writing the scheme of work for the new GCSE. His school, having been involved in the pilot, has now implemented the new GCSE.

Nathan Goodman (Physics) has an in-depth understanding of the new science specifications, thanks to his roles as Secondary Science Strategy Consultant for North East Lincolnshire LEA and Regional Coordinator at the Institute of Physics for the Physics Teacher Network. As an Assistant Headteacher, Nathan is involved in improving the teaching and learning of science at his school.

Dr Dorothy Warren (Chemistry) is a member of the Royal Society of Chemistry, a former science teacher, and a Secondary Science Consultant with the Quality and Improvement Service for North Yorkshire County Council. Having been involved in the pilot scheme for OCR Twenty First Century Science, she has an excellent understanding of the new specifications, which she has helped to implement in local schools.

Steve Langfield (Chemistry) has been a science teacher for over 20 years and is an experienced examiner and moderator. He currently works as a science coordinator at a designated Specialist Science School, at the forefront of innovation in science and mathematics.

This revision guide has been written and developed to help you get the most out of your revision.

This guide covers both Foundation and Higher Tier content.

HT Content that will only be tested on the Higher Tier papers appears in a pale yellow tinted box labelled with the **HT** symbol.

- The **coloured page headers** clearly identify the separate units, so that you can revise for each exam separately: Biology is red, Chemistry is purple, and Physics is blue.
- There are **practice questions** at the end of each unit so you can test yourself on what you've just learned. (The answers are given on pages 116–118 so you can mark your own answers.)

- You'll find **key words** in a yellow box on each two-page spread. They are also highlighted in colour within the text; Higher Tier key words are highlighted in orange. Make sure you know and understand all these words before moving on!
- There's a **glossary** at the back of the book. It contains all the key words from throughout the book so you can check any definitions you're not sure about.
- The **tick boxes** on the contents page let you track your revision progress: simply put a tick in the box next to each topic when you're confident that you know it.
- Don't just read the guide, **learn actively**! Constantly test yourself without looking at the text.

Good luck with your exams!

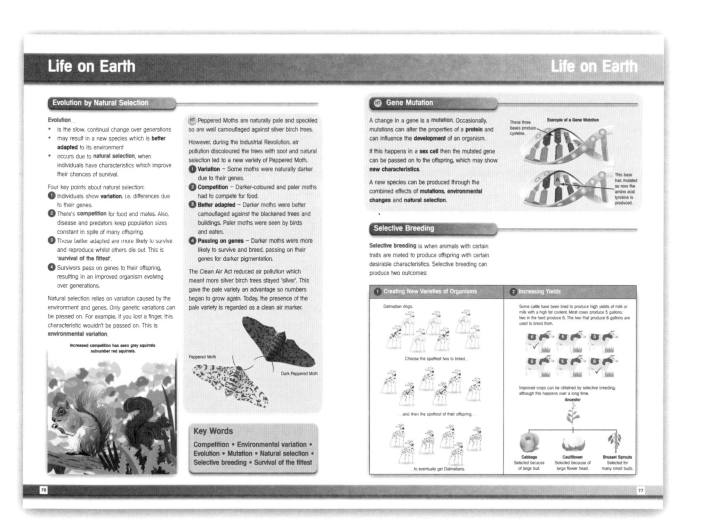

You and Your Genes

Variation

Differences between individuals of the same species are called **variation**.

Variation may be due to…
- **genetic factors**
- **environmental factors**.

Genetic Causes   Environmental Causes

Genetic Information

Genes carry the information needed for you to develop. **Different genes** control **different characteristics**, e.g. the colour of your eyes.

Genes…
- occur in long strings called **chromosomes**
- are located inside the **nucleus** of **every cell**.

Chromosomes are made of **DNA** (deoxyribonucleic acid) molecules. DNA molecules are…
- made up of **two strands**
- coiled to form a **double helix**.

DNA molecules form a complete set of instructions for…
- how the organism should be constructed
- how each cell should function.

Genes are sections of DNA. Genes **control the development** of different characteristics by **issuing instructions** to the cell. The cell carries out these instructions by producing **proteins**.

(HT) The proteins formed inside a cell can be…
- **structural proteins** (for cell growth or repair)
- **enzymes** (to speed up chemical reactions).

A Cell   A Section of One Chromosome

Gene for eye colour

One of four chromosomes — Nucleus

Genes for hair colour   Genes for height

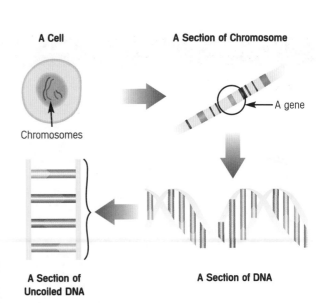

A Cell

Chromosomes

A Section of Chromosome

A gene

A Section of Uncoiled DNA   A Section of DNA

Genetic Modification

All organisms have DNA. This means it's possible to introduce genetic information from one organism into another. This will produce a new **combination** of genes and characteristics. It is called **genetic modification**.

Key Words

Allele • Chromosome • DNA • Gene • Nucleus • Protein • Variation

Chromosomes

Chromosomes normally come in **pairs**:

- Both chromosomes in a pair have the **same sequence** of genes, i.e. the same genes in the same place.
- Different species have different numbers of pairs. **Human cells** contain **23 pairs** of chromosomes (46 in total).

Sperm		Egg		Fertilised Egg Cell
	+		=	
23 chromosomes	+	23 chromosomes	=	46 chromosomes (23 pairs) – half from mother (egg) and half from father (sperm)

Sex cells contain single chromosomes. In humans they have a total of 23 chromosomes; half the number of a normal body cell.

Pairs of Chromosomes in a Human Male

1   2   3   4   5
6   7   8   9   10   11
12   13   14   15   16   17
18   19   20   21   22   XY

Alleles

A gene can have **different versions**, called **alleles**. For example, the gene for eye colour has two alleles: brown and blue. For each gene, you inherit one allele from your father and one from your mother. This is why you can have similarities to **both** of your parents.

You can inherit two alleles that are the same or two that are different. Brothers and sisters can **randomly inherit** different combinations for all the different genes, which is why they can be very different.

Alleles can be **dominant** or **recessive**.

Dominant allele – controls the development of a characteristic even if it's present on only one chromosome in a pair.

Recessive allele – controls the development of a characteristic only if a dominant allele isn't present, i.e. if the recessive allele is present on both chromosomes in a pair.

Genetic Diagrams

Genetic diagrams are used to show all the possible combinations of alleles and outcomes for a particular gene. They use...

- **capital letters** for **dominant** alleles
- **lower case letters** for **recessive** alleles.

You can also use a **family tree** to identify how you have inherited a characteristic, such as your hair colour.

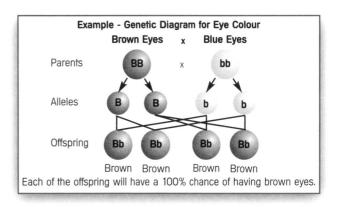

Example - Genetic Diagram for Eye Colour

	Brown Eyes	x	Blue Eyes
Parents	BB	x	bb
Alleles	B B		b b
Offspring	Bb Bb		Bb Bb
	Brown Brown		Brown Brown

Each of the offspring will have a 100% chance of having brown eyes.

You and Your Genes

Genetics and Lifestyle

Most characteristics are determined by several genes working together. However, they can be influenced by **environmental factors**. For example, your height is determined by a variety of genes, but factors like diet can also affect it.

Poor diet can lead to **disease**. For example, a fatty diet can increase the risk of heart disease.

It's possible to limit the chances of getting certain diseases by making **lifestyle changes**.

Sex Chromosomes

One of the 23 pairs of **chromosomes** in a human body cell is the **sex chromosomes**:

- In **females** the sex chromosomes are **identical**; they are both **X** chromosomes.
- In **males** they are **different**; there is an **X** and a **Y** chromosome. The Y chromosome is much shorter than the X chromosome.

HT The sex of an individual is determined by a gene on the **Y chromosome** called the **sex-determining region Y** (SRY) gene.

If the gene isn't present, i.e. if there are two **X chromosomes** present, the embryo will develop into a female.

If the gene is present, i.e. if there is an X chromosome and a Y chromosome, **testes** begin to develop.

After six weeks the testes start producing a hormone called **androgen**. Specialised **receptors** in the developing embryo detect the androgen and male reproductive organs begin to grow.

Sometimes the Y chromosome is present but androgen isn't detected. When this happens…

- the embryo develops female sex organs apart from the uterus
- the baby has a female body but is **infertile**.

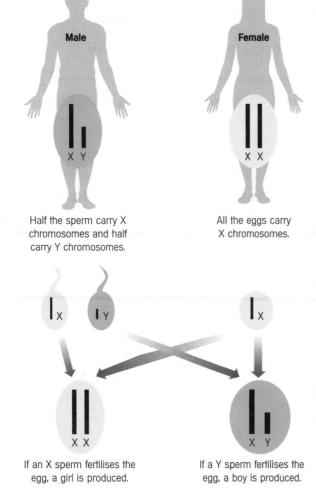

Male

X Y

Half the sperm carry X chromosomes and half carry Y chromosomes.

Female

X X

All the eggs carry X chromosomes.

X

Y

X

X X

If an X sperm fertilises the egg, a girl is produced.

X Y

If a Y sperm fertilises the egg, a boy is produced.

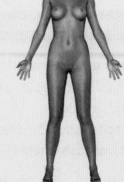

Androgen Detected
Genetically male.
Appears male.

Androgen not Detected
Genetically male.
Appears female but has no uterus.

Huntington's Disorder

Most characteristics are governed by a range of genes, so one 'faulty' **allele** may not affect the overall outcome. However, although rare, some disorders are caused by a single allele, e.g. **Huntington's disorder**.

Huntington's disorder (HD)…

- is a genetic disorder affecting the **central nervous system**. It's caused by a 'faulty' gene on the fourth pair of chromosomes
- damages the brain's **nerve cells**
- causes gradual changes, which develop into symptoms including **involuntary movement** and **dementia**
- is incurable, leading to premature death.

Symptoms of HD can **differ**, even within the same family. Symptoms normally develop in adulthood, which means sufferers may already have passed it on to their children. Only one parent needs to pass on the gene for a child to **inherit** it. Everyone who inherits the HD allele will develop the disorder because the allele is **dominant**.

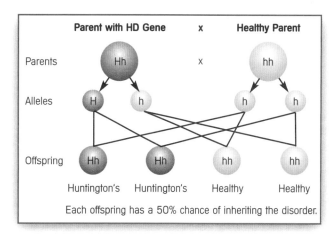

Each offspring has a 50% chance of inheriting the disorder.

Cystic Fibrosis

Cystic fibrosis affects **cell membranes**, causing a thick, sticky mucus, especially in the **lungs**, **gut** and **pancreas**.

Symptoms can include **weight loss, coughs, repeated chest infections, salty sweat** and **abnormal faeces**.

There's no cure, but scientists have identified the allele that causes it.

Unlike Huntington's disorder, the cystic fibrosis allele is **recessive**. So, if an individual has one **recessive allele**, they will not have the disorder's characteristics.

However, they are called **carriers** because they can pass the allele on to their children.

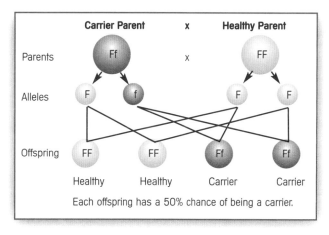

Each offspring has a 50% chance of being a carrier.

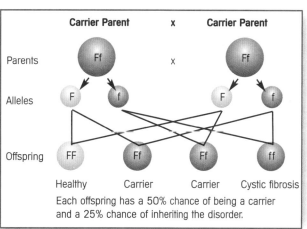

Each offspring has a 50% chance of being a carrier and a 25% chance of inheriting the disorder.

Key Words

Allele • Chromosome • Cystic fibrosis • Huntington's disorder • Sex-determining region Y

You and Your Genes

Genetic Testing

It's possible to test a person for a faulty **allele**. If the tests are positive, couples must choose whether to have children and risk passing on the disorder, to **adopt** a child instead, or to use **embryo selection**.

Fetuses can also be tested. If the faulty allele is present in a developing fetus, parents may decide whether to terminate the pregnancy.

Testing the Fetus

There are two ways of removing cells so that a **genetic test** can be carried out on a fetus.

Amniocentesis testing is carried out at 14–16 weeks.
1. A needle is inserted into the uterus, taking care to avoid the fetus.
2. A sample of **amniotic fluid**, carrying cells from the fetus, is extracted and tested.
3. If the test is positive, the pregnancy could be terminated.
4. There's a 0.5% chance of the test causing a miscarriage, and a small chance of infection.

Chorionic villus testing is carried out at 8–10 weeks.
1. A special catheter is inserted through the vagina and cervix until it reaches the **placenta**.
2. Part of the placenta has **chorionic villi**, which are made from **fetal cells**. Samples are removed and tested.
3. If the test is positive the pregnancy can be terminated much earlier than with amniocentesis testing.
4. The chance of miscarriage is much higher at 2%, but there's virtually no risk of infection.

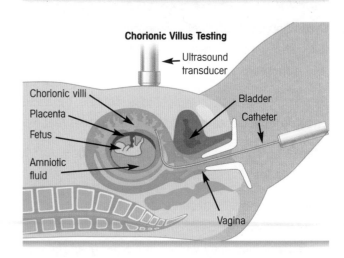

Amniocentesis Testing

- Amniotic fluid
- Placenta
- Fetus
- Uterus
- Cervix

Chorionic Villus Testing

- Ultrasound transducer
- Chorionic villi
- Placenta
- Fetus
- Amniotic fluid
- Bladder
- Catheter
- Vagina

Reliability

As no test is 100% reliable, genetic testing on a fetus can have a number of outcomes, as the table shows.

False negatives are rare and **false positives** even rarer. But a false positive result means that parents may choose to terminate the pregnancy when the fetus is in fact healthy.

Outcome	Test result	Reality
True Positive	Fetus **has** the disorder	Fetus **has** the disorder
True Negative	Fetus **does not** have the disorder	Fetus **does not** have the disorder
False Positive	Fetus **has** the disorder	Fetus **does not** have the disorder
False Negative	Fetus **does not** have the disorder	Fetus **has** the disorder

The Implications of Genetic Testing

Before genetic testing can become common practice, the following questions should be addressed:

- How can mistakes be prevented?
- Is it right to interfere with nature?
- Who has the right to decide if a disorder is worth living with?

HT There is always a difference between what **can** be done and what **should** be done. Governments may have the ability to test, but should they be allowed?

Potentially, genetic testing could be used to produce **genetic profiles** containing information such as…

- your **ethnicity**
- whether you're **susceptible** to certain conditions or diseases.

It's been suggested that babies could be **screened at birth**, allowing doctors…

- to tailor healthcare and prevent problems
- to stop genetic disorders from being passed on, eliminating them completely.

One view is that this would mean less suffering and the money currently spent on treatment could be used elsewhere. The **opposing view** is that these disorders are natural and it would be wrong to eliminate them.

Storing genetic information raises questions about **confidentiality**. For example, it could be used to **discriminate** and people may be turned down for jobs if they are found to have a **higher risk** of illness.

The availability of money and trained staff affects what can be done, so different countries develop different policies depending on their economy.

Embryo Selection

Embryo selection is another way of preventing babies from having genetic disorders. Embryos can be produced by *in vitro* **fertilisation** (IVF):

1. **Ova** are harvested from the mother and fertilised.
2. The embryos are tested for the faulty allele.
3. Healthy embryos are **implanted** into the **uterus**. The pregnancy proceeds as normal.

HT The procedure for embryo selection is called Pre-implantation Genetic Diagnosis (PGD):

1. After fertilisation the embryos are allowed to **divide** into 8 cells before a single cell is removed from each one for testing
2. The cells are tested to see if they carry the alleles for a **specific genetic disorder**.

Embryo selection is **controversial**:

- Some people believe it's **unnatural**.
- There are concerns that people could select certain characteristics, such as eye colour, sex, etc., in advance (pre-selection).

Pre-selection of a baby's characteristics could **reduce variation**. For example, if most people selected blue eyes for their baby, the brown eye allele could disappear in time.

Key Words

Allele • Fetus • Genetic test • *In vitro* fertilisation • Pre-implantation Genetic Diagnosis

You and Your Genes

Gene Therapy

Gene therapy…
- is a potential treatment for certain **genetic disorders**
- involves inserting 'healthy' genes into cells in order to treat a disease.

The most common method uses genes from healthy people.

The genes are inserted into a **modified virus**, which infects the patient. The genes become part of the patient's cells, correcting the faulty allele.

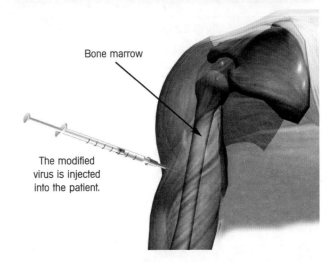

Bone marrow

The modified virus is injected into the patient.

Gene Therapy and Ethics

New procedures raise questions. Some **can** be answered by further **scientific research**, e.g:
- Does it work and is it safe? What are the potential risks and side effects?
- How do you target cells?
- Can gene therapy cause cancer?

Some questions **can't** be answered by science:
- Is it right to manipulate genes in this way?
- Where do we draw the line between repairing damage and making improvements?
- Do we have the right to decide for future generations?

These questions address the same **ethical** issue: **is gene therapy acceptable**? To answer this we need to decide what's right and what's wrong.

Society has **common beliefs**. For example, most people agree that murder is wrong. However, there are different views about what's acceptable, and about what should be done.

We shouldn't decide whether gene therapy is right or wrong by simply counting the arguments. The **quality** of each argument is more important. For example, you may believe it's more important to save lives than worry about an 'unnatural' procedure.

Decisions about ethical issues are normally based on what will **benefit the majority**. This means some people will always object to a decision.

Arguments For Gene Therapy	Arguments Against Gene Therapy
• It's an **acceptable procedure**, comparable to vaccination, and less invasive than surgery.	• It's **unnatural** and **morally wrong** to change people's genes and DNA.
• People with genetic conditions can need a lifetime of care and treatment. Gene therapy will **improve lives** and free up resources.	• It's **experimental** and we don't know the long-term effects.
• Some conditions reduce life expectancy. Gene therapy will allow a **normal life**.	• It will need to be tested on humans, which isn't safe as we don't know the **side effects**.

Asexual Reproduction

Bacteria and other **single-cell organisms** can reproduce by dividing to form two 'new' individuals. The new individuals are **clones** (genetically identical to the parent).

This is **asexual reproduction**. Most plants and some animals can reproduce in this way.

Variation in organisms that reproduce **asexually** is normally only caused by **environmental factors**.

Clones can occur naturally:
- The cells of an embryo sometimes **separate**.
- The two new embryos develop into **identical twins**.

HT **Animal clones** can be produced **artificially**:
- The **nucleus** from an adult body cell is transferred into an empty (nucleus removed) unfertilised egg cell.
- The new individual will have exactly the same genetic information as the donor.

Cell Division During Asexual Reproduction

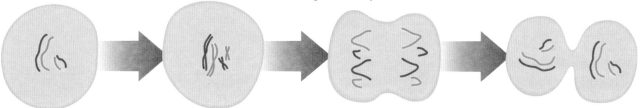

Parental cell with two pairs of chromosomes.

Each chromosome replicates itself.

The copies are pulled apart. Cell now divides for the only time.

Each 'daughter' cell has the same number of chromosomes and contains the same genes as the parental cell.

Stem Cells

Most organisms are made up of various **specialised** cells with **different structures**. In the early stages of development, cells aren't specialised. These are called **stem cells**.

Stem cells have the potential to develop into any type of cell. They can potentially be used to replace damaged tissues, e.g. in patients with **Parkinson's disease**.

To produce the number of stem cells needed for this type of treatment, it's necessary to **clone embryos**.

Stem cells are collected at the **8-cell stage** when cells are **specialised**. At the 16-cell stage specialisation begins. It's possible to still use cells up to the 150-cell stage. However, they aren't as **effective**.

The Ethical Issue

There's an **issue** as to whether it's right to clone embryos and extract stem cells. The debate is about whether these embryos should be seen as people. One view is that if an embryo is produced for IVF but not implanted, it no longer has a future. So, it's acceptable to use with parental consent.

It's been suggested that embryos could be cloned from the patient's cells. This is the first stage in **reproductive cloning** (a new individual identical to the donor), which is illegal in the UK.

Governments make **laws** on issues. **Special advisory committees** explore the **ethics** of procedures such as cloning and stem cell use.

Key Words

Asexual reproduction • Clone • Ethics • Gene therapy • Stem cell

Module B1 Summary

Variation and Genetic Information

Variation = differences between individuals of the same species, due to **genetic** or **environmental** factors.

Genes…
- are sections of **DNA** (deoxyribonucleic acid) in **chromosomes**
- are located inside the **nucleus**
- carry the information needed for you to develop
- issue instructions to the cell to make **proteins**.

Alleles = different versions of a gene:
- **Dominant** – control a characteristic if present.
- **Recessive** – control a characteristic if it's present on both chromosomes.

HT **Proteins** inside a cell can be **structural** or **enzymes**.

Chromosomes

Chromosomes…
- are made of DNA
- normally come in pairs. (Both pairs have the same gene sequence.)

Human sex cells contain single chromosomes.

There are two sex chromosomes – X and Y:
- **XX** chromosomes = girl
- **XY** chromosomes = boy.

HT The sex of an individual is determined by a gene on the Y chromosome called the **sex-determining region Y** gene.

Genetic diagrams and **family trees** ➡ Used to identify how you inherit a characteristic.

Genetic Disorders

A fetus can be **genetically tested** for a **faulty allele** by **amniocentisis** testing and **chorionic villus** testing.

Embryo selection is…
- used to prevent babies having genetic disorders (IVF)
- controversial.

Disorder	Part of Body Affected	Cause
Huntington's	Central nervous system	Dominant allele
Cystic fibrosis	Cell membranes	Recessive allele

HT **Pre-implantation genetic diagnosis** – cells are tested for a specific genetic disorder.

Gene Therapy

Gene therapy ➡ **healthy genes** inserted into cells to treat a disease.

Gene therapy could be used as a **potential treatment** for genetic disorders.

Gene therapy raises **ethical questions** – people may see it as an **'unnatural'** procedure.

Clones

Asexual reproduction = single cell organisms **divide** to form two new individuals.

Bacteria and other **single-cell organisms** can reproduce asexually.

Clones = new individuals identical to the parent.

Clones can occur naturally to form **identical twins**.

(HT) **Animal clones** can be produced **artificially**.

Stem Cells

Most organisms are made of **specialised cells** with **different structures**.

Stem cells…
- are cells in the early stages of development that are not yet **specialised**
- have the potential to develop into **any type** of cell
- have the potential to **replace damaged** tissues.

There's an **issue** as to whether it's right or wrong to clone embryos and use stem cells.

Genetics and Ethics

Ethical questions (e.g. Is it right to interfere?) need to be addressed before genetic testing becomes common.

Special advisory committees advise the government which makes laws on the ethics of such procedures.

Decisions about ethical questions are normally based on what will **benefit** the **majority**.

There will always be people who **object** to a decision.

(HT) There is a danger that **storing genetic information** could be used to **discriminate**.

Governments may have the ability to test, but should they be allowed to?

There is a difference between what **can** be done and what **should** be done.

1 Circle the correct option in the following sentence:

A gene provides instructions to make **chromosomes / proteins / nuclei / cells**.

HT **2** What are the two types of protein formed inside cells?

a) _____

b) _____

3 Fill in the missing word to complete the sentence below:

Different versions of the same gene are called _____ .

4 Complete the genetic diagram below.

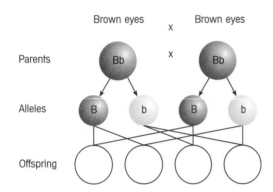

Brown eyes   X   Brown eyes

X

Parents   Bb   Bb

Alleles   B   b   B   b

Offspring

5 Niamh is growing yeast, a single-celled fungus, in an experiment. She adds a small sample of the yeast to a growth mixture. After a few days there's more yeast in the flask than she had to start with.

Use the words below to complete the following sentences.

asexual	X	sexual	Y	genetic
Z	environmental	chromosomes	nucleus	clones

a) The cells that make up Niamh's skin contain 23 pairs of _____ .

b) Yeast reproduces via _____ reproduction.

c) All the yeast are genetically identical, therefore they are _____ .

d) The yeast don't look exactly the same. This is due to _____ factors.

e) Niamh was produced by _____ reproduction.

f) Niamh is female because she inherited an X chromosome from her father and a _____ chromosome from her mother.

6 a) Which part of the body does Huntington's disorder affect?

....

b) Name two symptoms of…

i) Huntington's disorder ....

ii) Cystic fibrosis ....

7 There are two ways of removing cells so that a genetic test can be carried out on a fetus to see if it has a genetic disorder. Name them and circle the test which takes place at 8–10 weeks of pregnancy.

....

8 The table below is jumbled. Draw lines from each outcome to the correct test result and reality. One line has been drawn for you.

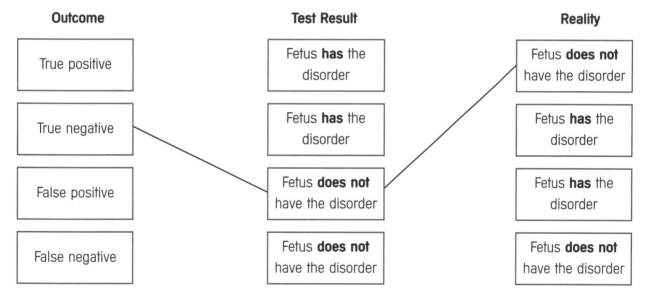

Outcome	Test Result	Reality
True positive	Fetus **has** the disorder	Fetus **does not** have the disorder
True negative	Fetus **has** the disorder	Fetus **has** the disorder
False positive	Fetus **does not** have the disorder	Fetus **has** the disorder
False negative	Fetus **does not** have the disorder	Fetus **does not** have the disorder

9 Fill in the missing words to complete the sentence below:

Bacteria and other .... organisms can .... by

.... to form two new individuals.

10 Complete and label the diagram below to show how 'daughter' cells are formed.

Parental cell with two pairs of chromosomes.   Each chromosome replicates itself.   ....

Air Quality

Pollutants in the Air

Pollutants are chemicals. They can harm the **environment** and our **health**.

Human actions such as burning **fossil fuels** release pollutants into the **atmosphere**, e.g. from power stations or cars.

Pollutants can harm us indirectly. For example, **acid rain** makes rivers too acidic for organisms to survive. This affects our **food chain** and **natural resources**, e.g. trees.

Pollutant	Harmful to...	Why?
Carbon dioxide	• Environment	• Traps heat in the Earth's atmosphere (it is a greenhouse gas.)
Nitrogen oxides	• Environment • Humans	• Causes acid rain. • Causes breathing problems and can make asthma worse.
Sulfur dioxide	• Environment	• Causes acid rain.
Particulates (small particles of solids, e.g. carbon)	• Environment • Humans	• Makes buildings dirty. • Can make asthma and lung infections worse if inhaled.
Carbon monoxide	• Humans	• Prevents the blood from carrying oxygen, which can be fatal.

The Atmosphere

The Earth is surrounded by a **thin layer of gases** called the **atmosphere**.

The atmosphere contains...
- about 78% **nitrogen**
- 21% **oxygen**
- 1% **argon** and other **noble gases**
- small amounts of **water vapour**, **carbon dioxide**, and **other gases**.

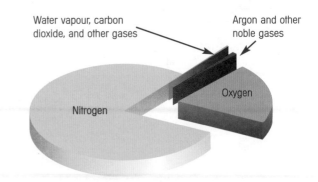

Measuring Pollutants

It's possible to measure **concentrations** of pollutants in the air in **ppb (parts per billion)** or **ppm (parts per million)**. For example, a **sulfur dioxide** concentration of 16ppb means that in every one billion (1 000 000 000) molecules of air, 16 molecules will be sulfur dioxide.

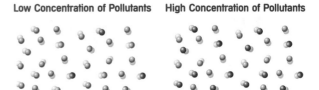

The red circles represent pollutant molecules.

Pollution Data

Data can **test a theory** or an **explanation**.

Carbon monoxide (CO) is an example of a pollutant caused by humans. **Concentrations** are likely to be higher in populated areas, e.g. cities.

The following data was collected in two places on the same day with a CO meter:

Time	City Centre Concentration	Country Park Concentration
9.00am	5.2	0.2
10.00am	4.9	0.1
11.00am	5.0	0.1
12.00pm	2.6	0.0
1.00pm	4.8	0.1

Measurements like this vary because...
- **variables**, like the volume of traffic, affect concentrations
- measuring equipment has **limited accuracy** and can be affected by the user's skill.

It's not possible to give a **true value** for the CO concentration. It is likely to be in the middle of the range of values.

Outliers are values that...
- are very different from the rest
- fall **well outside** other measurements and normally indicate **error**.

The measurement of 2.6ppm would be excluded from the city's data because it's an **outlier**. It may be an outlier because the user misread the scale; it's unlikely that traffic would decrease at midday.

It's important to repeat measurements because one on its own is unreliable. Errors should stand out when analysing repeated measurements.

Calculating the Mean

Finding the **mean** (average) from repeated measurements can overcome variations and give a **best estimate**.

Mean	$=$	$\dfrac{\text{Sum of all values}}{\text{Number of values}}$	Do not use outliers in mean calculations!

$$\text{City mean} = \frac{5.2 + 4.9 + 5.0 + 4.8}{4} = 5.0\text{ppm}$$

$$\text{Country mean} = \frac{0.2 + 0.1 + 0.1 + 0.0 + 0.1}{5} = 0.1\text{ppm}$$

The mean CO concentration in the city is significantly higher than in the country park. This supports the theory that CO is a pollutant caused by human activity.

HT There's a **real difference** between the mean CO concentrations in the city and park. This is because the difference between the mean values is **greater** than the range of each set of data.

If the difference between the values had been **smaller** than the range then there would have been **no real difference**.

The result would have been insignificant so the data wouldn't support the theory.

Key Words

Atmosphere • Concentration • Outlier • Pollutant • Variable

Air Quality

Chemicals

Elements are the **'building blocks'** of **all** materials. There are over 100 elements. Each one is made of tiny **particles** called **atoms**.

All atoms of a particular element are the same and **unique** to that element. Atoms can **join together** to form bigger building blocks called **molecules**.

Compounds form when the atoms of two or more different elements **chemically combine** to form molecules. Compounds are very different from the properties of the elements they are made from.

Chemical symbols and **numbers** are used to write **formulae**. A formula shows the...

- different elements that make a compound
- number of atoms of each element in one molecule.

Example – A water molecule, H_2O.

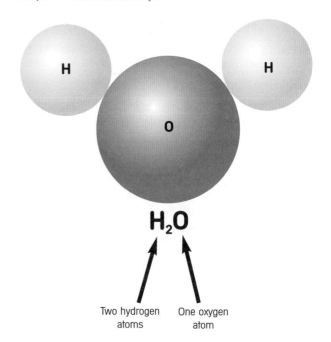

$$H_2O$$

Two hydrogen atoms — One oxygen atom

Chemical Change

Chemical reactions form **new substances** from old ones. Atoms in the **reactants** (starting substances) are rearranged to make **products**:

- Joined atoms may be separated.
- Separate atoms may be joined.
- Joined atoms may be separated and then joined again in different ways.

These changes are **not** easily reversible.

Word equations show what happens during a chemical reaction. The **reactants** are on one side and the **products** (newly formed chemicals) on the other:

Reactants	⟶	Products

No atoms are lost or produced during a chemical reaction, so there will always be the **same number** of atoms on each side.

Combustion

Combustion is a chemical reaction. Combustion occurs when fuel burns and energy is released. For combustion to take place, oxygen must be present.

Coal is mainly made up of **carbon**. This equation shows what happens when coal is burned.

The equation tells us that one atom of carbon (solid) and one molecule of oxygen (gas) produces one molecule of carbon dioxide (gas).

Carbon	+	Oxygen	⟶	Carbon dioxide
C(s)	+	O_2(g)	⟶	CO_2(g)
C	+	O O	⟶	O C O

Complete Combustion

Complete combustion occurs when there's enough oxygen present for fuel to burn completely. Petrol, diesel and fuel oil consist mainly of compounds called **hydrocarbons** which...

- contain only **hydrogen** and **carbon** atoms
- produce carbon dioxide and water (**hydrogen oxide**) when burned in air.

Methane	+	Oxygen	$\longrightarrow$	Carbon dioxide	+	Water
$CH_4(g)$	+	$2O_2(g)$	$\longrightarrow$	$CO_2(g)$	+	$2H_2O(l)$

Incomplete Combustion

Incomplete combustion occurs when fuel is burned and there's not enough oxygen. Depending on the amount of oxygen present, **carbon** (C) **particulates** or **carbon monoxide** (CO) may be produced.

Methane	+	Oxygen	$\longrightarrow$	Carbon	+	Water
$CH_4(g)$	+	$O_2(g)$	$\longrightarrow$	$C(s)$	+	$2H_2O(l)$

Methane	+	Oxygen	$\longrightarrow$	Carbon monoxide	+	Water
$2CH_4(g)$	+	$3O_2(g)$	$\longrightarrow$	$2CO(g)$	+	$4H_2O(l)$

Incomplete combustion occurs in car engines. Exhaust emissions contain carbon particulates and carbon monoxide as well as carbon dioxide.

Coal can contain **sulfur**, so **sulfur dioxide** is released when it's burned:

Sulfur	+	Oxygen	$\longrightarrow$	Sulfur dioxide
$S(g)$	+	$O_2(g)$	$\longrightarrow$	$SO_2(g)$

Key Words

Atom • Combustion • Compound • Element • Hydrocarbon • Product • Reactant

Air Quality

HT Incomplete Combustion (cont.)

During the combustion of fuels, high temperatures e.g. in a car engine, can cause **nitrogen** in the atmosphere to react with **oxygen**. This produces **nitrogen monoxide** (NO).

Nitrogen	+	Oxygen	⟶	Nitrogen monoxide
$N_2(g)$	+	$O_2(g)$	⟶	$2NO(g)$
N N	+	O O	⟶	N O / N O

Nitrogen monoxide is then **oxidised** to produce **nitrogen dioxide** (NO_2):

Nitrogen monoxide	+	Oxygen	⟶	Nitrogen dioxide
$2NO(g)$	+	$O2(g)$	⟶	$2NO_2(g)$
N O / N O	+	O O	⟶	O N O / O N O

When NO and NO_2 occur together they are called **NOx**.

Effects of Pollutants

Once pollutants are released into the atmosphere they have to go somewhere as they can't just disappear. This is when they start causing **environmental problems**.

Carbon is **deposited** on surfaces such as stone buildings, making them dirty.

Some **carbon dioxide** is removed by **natural processes**:

- It is needed by plants for **photosynthesis**.
- Some **dissolves in rain** and **sea water**, where it **reacts** with other chemicals.

We **produce too much** carbon dioxide so it's not all used up naturally. It stays in the atmosphere, so carbon dioxide levels **increase** each year.

Carbon dioxide is a **greenhouse gas**. It is contributing to global warming, which is leading to **climate change**.

Sulfur dioxide and **nitrogen dioxide** dissolve in water to produce **acid rain**, which damages trees, corrodes metal and upsets the pH balance of rivers, causing plants and animals to die.

Key Words

Acid rain • Allergy • Greenhouse gas

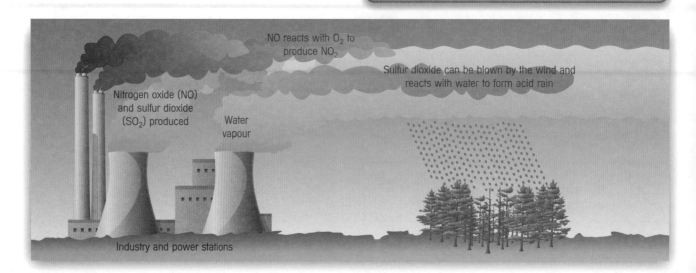

NO reacts with O_2 to produce NO_2

Nitrogen oxide (NO) and sulfur dioxide (SO_2) produced

Water vapour

Sulfur dioxide can be blown by the wind and reacts with water to form acid rain

Industry and power stations

Identifying Health Hazards

To find out how air quality affects us, scientists look for **correlations** that might link a **factor** (e.g. a pollutant in the air) to an **outcome** (e.g. a respiratory complaint like asthma).

Example – Hayfever

Studies have proved that pollen causes hayfever.

Records have shown most cases occur in summer when pollen counts are high. However, this correlation wasn't conclusive evidence as other variables could influence the outcome, e.g. temperature, other pollutants.

Skin tests were carried out too. Pollen was stuck to the skin using plasters.

In some volunteers the skin became red and inflamed, indicating **allergic reaction**. The study showed...
* that people with pollen **allergy** also had hayfever
* those who **didn't** have pollen allergy **didn't** get hayfever.

This provided stronger evidence of a link between pollen and hayfever.

> HT **Repeated** skin tests always produced the **same results**, which proved the tests were **reliable**.

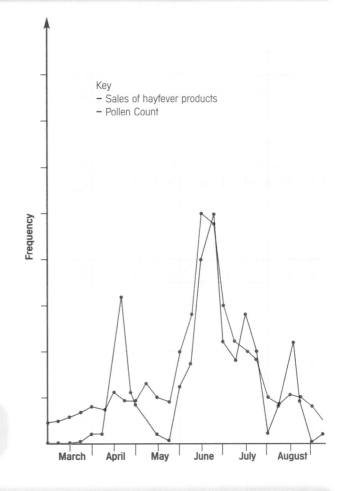

Key
- Sales of hayfever products
- Pollen Count

HT Example – Asthma

Asthma is another condition linked to **air quality**. However, this example is more complicated.

Studies have shown that when the **concentration** of **NO$_2$** (nitrogen dioxide) increases, **more** asthma attacks are triggered.

People still have attacks when levels are **very low**. This suggests that although NO$_2$ can increase the chance of an attack, it's not the primary cause.

Many factors can trigger an attack. Scientists need to study a large sample to understand what factors cause and aggravate asthma.

Air Quality

Improving Air Quality

Cars and power stations **burning fossil fuels** are **two major sources** of **atmospheric pollution**. Emissions from these sources need to be reduced.

Power Station Pollution

Power station emissions can be reduced by…

- using **less electricity**
- a filter system to **remove** sulfur dioxide and particulates (carbon and ash) from flue gases before they leave the chimney
- **removing toxic chemicals** from gas and oil before burning
- using **alternative renewable sources**, e.g. **solar**, **wind** and **hydroelectric** energy.

Car Pollution

About half of the UK's CO emissions are produced by road transport.

Car emissions can be reduced by…

- using **low sulfur** fuel in a car with a modern **fuel-efficient** engine
- buying a hybrid car, which uses electricity and petrol
- **converting** the engine to run on biodiesel, a **renewable fuel**
- using public transport
- making sure cars have **catalytic converters**, which **reduce** carbon monoxide and nitrogen monoxide in the engine exhaust gases.

The following formulae show the reactions that occur in a catalytic converter:

Carbon monoxide	+	Oxygen	→	Carbon dioxide
$CO(g)$	+	$O_2(g)$	→	$CO_2(g)$

Nitrogen monoxide	+	Carbon monoxide	→	Nitrogen	+	Carbon dioxide
$2NO(g)$	+	$2CO(g)$	→	$N_2(g)$	+	$2CO_2(g)$

The only way to reduce emissions is to **burn less** fossil fuels.

Global Choices

In 1997 an international meeting about climate change in Kyoto, Japan, set **targets** to lower emissions for individual countries.

Each country's government must take appropriate measures to meet its target.

National Choices

Government **rules** and **regulations** include…

- **legal limits** for **exhaust emissions**, enforced by MOT tests
- **compulsory** catalytic converters
- subsidies or reduced taxes for companies who use 'cleaner' fuels
- introducing a **tax system** that encourages you to buy smaller cars
- encouraging investment in **non-polluting renewable energy**.

These laws impact on science and industry. For example, when new cars are developed the technology must meet **legal requirements**.

Some governments are concerned that these steps will mean a decline in manufacturing, employment and the national economy.

Local Choices

Local authorities may provide **environmentally friendly** choices. For example…

- door-step **recycling** collections (e.g. for paper, bottles)
- regular buses or trains
- electric trams (in some cities)
- cycle paths.

Personal Choices

Individual choices we make affect the amount of air pollution. For example…

- **using less energy** reduces demand, e.g. not leaving televisions on standby
- alternative transport, e.g. cycling **cuts emissions** and keeps you fit.

Recycling materials…

- helps **conserve** natural resources
- **saves** energy, e.g. 95% less energy is used to recycle a can than is used to make a new one.

Module C1 Summary

Pollutants in the Air

Pollutants…
- are **harmful chemicals** in the air
- are caused by **human activity** − burning fossil fuels
- cause **acid rain, breathing problems** and **global warming**.

Pollution Data

Data can **test** or **explain** a theory.

Concentrations of CO are **higher** in populated areas ➡ Concentration of pollutants measured in **ppb** or **ppm**.

Measurements are affected by…
- **variables** (e.g. volume of traffic)
- a user's **skill**
- the **accuracy** of measuring equipment.

An **outlier** is a measurement that stands out − it's **very different** from the other data and can indicate **error**.

It's important to **repeat** measurements to get a **reliable** result. Finding the mean gives a **best estimate**.

$$\text{Mean} = \frac{\text{Sum of all values}}{\text{Number of values}}$$

Chemicals in the Air

Earth's atmosphere is…
- 78% **nitrogen**
- 21% **oxygen**
- 1% **argon** and other **noble gases**
- small amounts of **other gases** e.g. carbon dioxide.

Chemicals

Elements…
- are the building blocks of all materials
- are made of **particles** called **atoms**.

All atoms of a particular element are the **same** and **unique to that element** ➡ Atoms join to form **molecules**.

Compounds = atoms of two different elements **chemically combined** to form molecules.

Chemical symbols and **numbers** are used to write **formulae**.

A **formula** shows the…
- **different elements** that make a **compound**
- number of **atoms** of each **element** in **one molecule**.

Chemical Change

Chemical reactions form **new substances (products)** from old ones ➡ Changes are **not** easily reversible.

Reactants ➡ Products

No atoms are **lost** or **produced** during a reaction.

Combustion

Combustion = fuels burn and energy is released.

Complete combustion = plenty of oxygen must be present.

Petrol, diesel and **fuel oil** = mainly **compounds** called **hydrocarbons**.

Hydrocarbons…
- contain only **hydrogen** and **carbon** atoms
- produce carbon dioxide and water when burned in air.

Incomplete Combustion

Incomplete combustion = not enough oxygen for fuel to burn completely ➡ **Carbon particulates** or **carbon monoxide** are produced ➡ Occurs in car engines.

Coal = mainly carbon. Can contain sulfur ➡ sulfur dioxide is released when it's burned.

HT **Nitrogen monoxide** – produced when high temperatures during fuel combustion cause nitrogen to **react** with oxygen.

Nitrogen monoxide **oxidises** to produce **nitrogen dioxide** ➡ Oxides of nitrogen are called **NOx**.

Pollutants and Air Quality

Pollutants cause **environmental problems**, e.g. carbon dioxide is a **greenhouse gas** ➡ Contributes to **global warming**.

Some carbon dioxide is removed by **photosynthesis**; some **dissolves** in rain and sea water.

Human activity produces **too much** carbon dioxide ➡ It stays in the atmosphere and **levels increase**.

Sulfur dioxide + **nitrogen dioxide** + **water** = acid rain.

Cars and **power stations** burn fossil fuels = major sources of pollution ➡ Emissions can be **reduced** (e.g. by using **alternative renewable energy, catalytic converters**).

Governments make **laws** to reduce emissions. **Local authorities** may provide **choices** e.g. regular buses. **Individuals** can make **choices** e.g. **recycling**.

Module C1 Practice Questions

1 Circle the correct option in the following sentences:

a) The main gas in the atmosphere is **nitrogen / oxygen / argon / helium**.

b) 21% of the atmosphere is made up of **nitrogen / oxygen / argon / helium**.

2 What is an outlier?

....

3 Floyd used a meter to measure the concentration of carbon dioxide at the side of a busy road. Here are the results for 9am:

Reading	1	2	3	4	5
Concentration (ppm)	350	220	355	360	355

a) Why did he repeat the measurement? ....

b) Which result is the outlier? ....

c) Write the equation used to calculate the mean.

....

d) Calculate the mean of Floyd's measurements, not including the outlier.

....

....

4 Petrol and diesel are made from compounds of which two elements? Tick the two correct options.

A Oxygen ⬭

B Methane ⬭

C Carbon ⬭

D Hydrogen ⬭

E Nitrogen ⬭

F Helium ⬭

5 Complete the following equation for the complete combustion of methane gas:

Methane	+	Oxygen	→	.... + ...
$CH_4(g)$	+	$2O_2(g)$	→	.... + ...
H–C(H)(H)H	+	O=O O=O	→	.... + ...

6 If a burning fuel contains 200 atoms of carbon, how many atoms of carbon will there be in the materials made by the reaction?

_____

7 Fill in the missing words to complete the sentences below:

Carbon dioxide gas is produced by burning _____ . Plants use some of the carbon

dioxide for _____ , some of the carbon dioxide _____ in rain and sea

water and some stays in the air, increasing the _____ .

8 a) What is the main element in coal?

_____

b) What happens to the sulfur in coal when it burns?

_____

c) What problem can this cause in the environment?

_____

HT 9 What type of reaction is the conversion of nitrogen monoxide to nitrogen dioxide in air?

_____

10 Without changing the amount of coal burned, name two factors a power station could change to reduce its harmful emissions.

a) _____

b) _____

11 What measures can an individual take to reduce air pollution? Tick the five correct options.

A Make sure car engines are fuel-efficient	◯	**B** Use low sulfur fuel	◯
C Incinerate	◯	**D** Burn more fossil fuels	◯
E Use public transport	◯	**F** Buy a car with a bigger engine	◯
G Recycle	◯	**H** Fit a catalytic converter	◯

The Earth in the Universe

The Earth

When it first formed, Earth was completely **molten** (hot liquid). Scientists estimate Earth is **4500 million** years old as it has to be older than its oldest rocks.

> (HT) The oldest rocks found on Earth are about 4000 million years old.

Studying rocks tells us more about the Earth's structure and how it has changed as a result of the following processes:

- **Erosion** – the Earth's surface is made of **rock layers,** one on top of another. The oldest is at the bottom. The layers are **compacted sediment**, produced by weathering and erosion. Erosion changes the surface over time.

- **Craters** – the moon's surface is covered with **impact craters** from meteors. Meteors also hit the Earth but craters have been erased by erosion.
- **Mountain formation** – if new mountains weren't being formed the Earth's surface would have eroded down to sea level.
- **Folding** – some rocks look as if they have been folded in half. This would require huge force over a long time; further evidence the Earth is very old.

Further evidence can be found by studying…

- **fossils** of plants and animals in **sedimentary rock layers**, which show how life's changed
- the **radioactivity** of rocks. All rocks are **radioactive**, but their radioactivity decreases over time. Radioactive dating measures radiation levels to find out a rock's age.

The Structure of the Earth

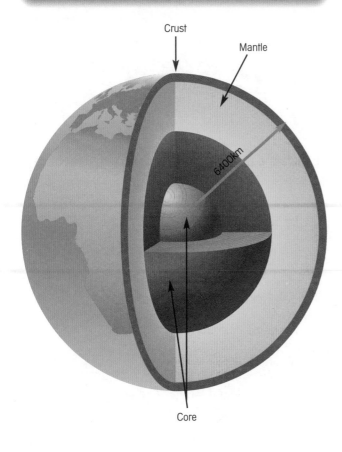

Crust

Mantle

6400km

Core

Thin rocky crust:
- Thickness varies between 10km and 100km.
- Oceanic crust lies beneath the oceans.
- Continental crust forms continents.

The mantle:
- Extends almost halfway to the centre.
- Has a higher density, and different composition, than rock in the crust.
- Very hot, but under pressure.

The core:
- Over half of the Earth's radius.
- Made of nickel and iron and has a liquid outer part and solid inner part.
- The decay of radioactive elements inside the Earth releases energy, keeping the interior hot.

> ## Key Words
>
> **Continental drift • Erosion • Geohazard • Peer review • Tectonic plate**

Continental Drift

Continental drift theory was proposed by **Wegener**. He saw that the continents had a jigsaw fit, with mountain ranges and rock patterns **matching up**.

There were also fossils of the same animals on different continents. He said that different continents had separated and drifted apart. Wegener also claimed that when two continents collided they forced each other upwards to make mountains.

Geologists didn't accept Wegener's theory because…
- he wasn't a geologist so was seen as an outsider
- the supporting evidence was limited
- it could be explained more simply, e.g. a bridge connecting continents had eroded over time
- the movement of the continents was not detectable.

Evidence from seafloor spreading finally convinced the scientific community that Wegener was correct. Through this **peer review** process it became an accepted theory.

How The Earth Once Was

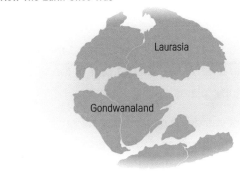

How The Earth Looks Today

Tectonic Plates

Earth's crust is cracked into several large pieces called **tectonic plates**. The plates…
- float on the Earth's **mantle** as they're less dense
- can move apart, move towards, or slide past each other.

The lines where plates meet are called **plate boundaries**. **Volcanoes**, **earthquakes** and **mountain formations** normally occur there.

Earthquakes near coastlines or at sea can often result in a **tsunami** (a tidal wave).

Geohazards

A **geohazard** is a **natural hazard**, e.g. floods, hurricanes. Some have warning signs which give authorities time to evacuate the area, use sandbags, etc.

However, others strike without warning so **precautionary measures** need to be taken.

For example…
- buildings in earthquake zones are designed to withstand tremors
- authorities will often refuse planning permission in areas prone to flooding.

The Earth in the Universe

Seafloor Spreading

The **mantle** is fairly solid just below the Earth's crust. Further down it is **liquid**.

Convection currents in the mantle cause **magma** to rise. The currents move the solid part of the mantle and the tectonic plates.

Where the plates are moving apart, magma reaches the surface and **hardens**, forming new areas of **oceanic crust** (seafloor) and pushing the existing floor outwards.

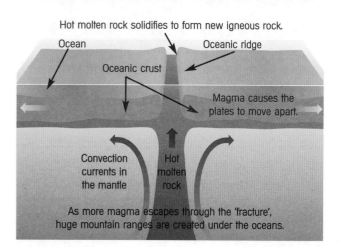

Hot molten rock solidifies to form new igneous rock.

Ocean

Oceanic ridge

Oceanic crust

Magma causes the plates to move apart.

Convection currents in the mantle

Hot molten rock

As more magma escapes through the 'fracture', huge mountain ranges are created under the oceans.

HT Plate Tectonics

New crust is **continuously forming** at the crest of an oceanic ridge and old rock is pushed out. This causes seafloors to spread by approximately 10cm a year.

Earth has a **magnetic field**. It changes polarity every million years. Combined with the seafloor spreading, this produces **rock stripes** of **alternating polarity**. Geologists can see how quickly crust is forming by the width of the stripes. This occurs at **constructive plate boundaries** where plates are moving apart.

When oceanic and continental plates **collide**, the denser oceanic plate is forced under the continental plate. This is **subduction**. The oceanic plate melts and molten rock can rise to form volcanoes. This occurs at **destructive plate boundaries**.

Mountain ranges form along colliding plate boundaries as sedimentary rock is forced up by the pressure created in a collision.

Earthquakes occur most frequently at plate boundaries, when plates slide past each other or collide:

- Pressure builds up as plates push on each other.
- Eventually, **stored energy** is released and waves of energy spread from the **epicentre**.

Plate movement is crucial in the rock cycle:

- Old rock is destroyed through **subduction.**
- **Igneous rock** is formed when magma reaches the surface.
- Plate collisions can produce high temperatures and pressure, causing the rock to fold.
- **Sedimentary rock** becomes **metamorphic rock.**

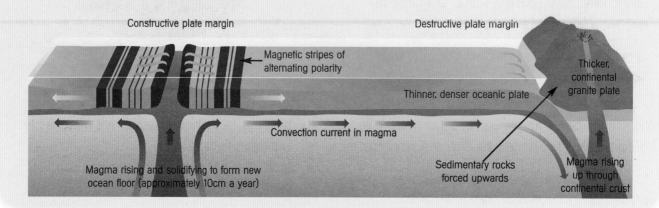

Constructive plate margin

Destructive plate margin

Magnetic stripes of alternating polarity

Thicker, continental granite plate

Thinner, denser oceanic plate

Convection current in magma

Magma rising and solidifying to form new ocean floor (approximately 10cm a year)

Sedimentary rocks forced upwards

Magma rising up through continental crust

The Solar System

HT The **Solar System** was formed about 5000 million years ago.

1 The Solar System started as **dust** and **gas clouds**, pulled together by gravity.

2 This created intense heat. **Nuclear fusion** began and the Sun (a star) was born.

3 The remaining dust and gas formed smaller masses, which were **attracted** to the Sun.

Smaller masses in our Solar System are:

- **Planets** – nine large masses that orbit the Sun.
- **Moons** – small masses orbiting planets.
- **Asteroids** – small, rocky masses that orbit the Sun.
- **Comets** – small, icy masses orbiting the Sun.

Planets, moons and asteroids all move in **elliptical** (slightly squashed circular) orbits.

Comets move in **highly elliptical** orbits. Earth takes **one year** to make a **complete orbit**.

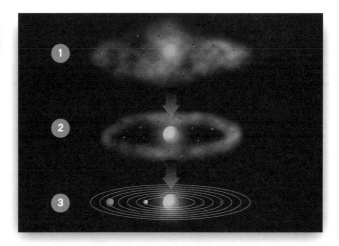

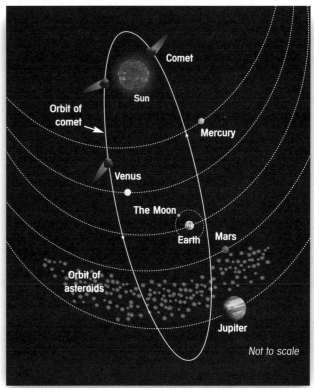

The Sun

The Sun is only **500 million years older** than Earth.

The Sun's energy comes from **nuclear fusion**:

- Hydrogen atoms **fuse** together to produce an atom with a **larger mass**, i.e. a new chemical element.
- **Trapped energy** in hydrogen atoms is **released**.

All the chemical elements larger than helium were formed by nuclear fusion in earlier stars.

HT It is the **nuclei** of hydrogen atoms that fuse together during nuclear fusion.

Key Words

Convection current • Gravity • Magnetic field • Nuclear fusion • Subduction

The Earth in the Universe

The Universe

The Universe is much older than the Sun, approximately **14 000 million years** old.

Not to scale

The Universe – contains billions of galaxies, with vast distances between them.

Our Sun

Our star – the Sun, 100 times wider than Earth

Our galaxy

Our galaxy – the Milky Way, 100 000 light years across, containing at least 200 billion stars.

Our planet – the Earth, 12 800km in diameter

The Speed of Light

Light travels at very high but **finite** (limited) speeds. If the distance is great enough, **light speed** can be measured.

HT The **speed of light** is **300 000km/s** (around 1 million times faster than sound). Light from Earth takes just over 1 second to reach the Moon (approximately 384 400km).

Sunlight takes 8 minutes to reach Earth. When we look at the Sun we see it as it was 8 minutes earlier.

Vast space distances are measured in **light years**. One light year is the distance light travels in one year (approximately 9500 billion km).

The nearest galaxy to the **Milky Way** is 2.2 million light years away.

Measuring Distances in Space

Distances are measured in **two** ways:

1. **Relative brightness** – the **dimmer** a star, the **further away** it is. However, brightness can vary so its distance is never certain.

2. **Parallax** – if you hold a finger at arm's length and close each eye in turn, your finger appears to move. The closer your finger, the more it seems to move. Parallax uses this idea to work out distance. Stars in the near distance appear to move against the background of distant stars. The closer they are, the more they appear to move. The further the star, the less accurate the measurement is.

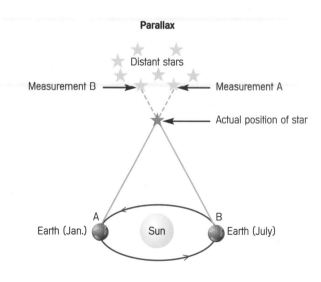

Parallax

Distant stars

Measurement B →   ← Measurement A

← Actual position of star

A   B
Earth (Jan.)   Sun   Earth (July)

Distant Stars

Radiation from stars tells us what we know about them. Types of radiation that stars produce include **visible light**, **ultraviolet** and **infrared**.

Light pollution is when lights on Earth make it difficult to see the stars. The Hubble Space Telescope orbits at 600km, so it's not affected by this.

The Life Cycle of a Star

All stars consist of hydrogen and have a **finite life**:

- When a star's hydrogen supply eventually runs out, it **swells** and becomes **colder**.
- It forms a **red giant** or a **red super giant**, depending on its size.

Key Words

Light speed • Light year • Neutron star • Radiation • Supernova

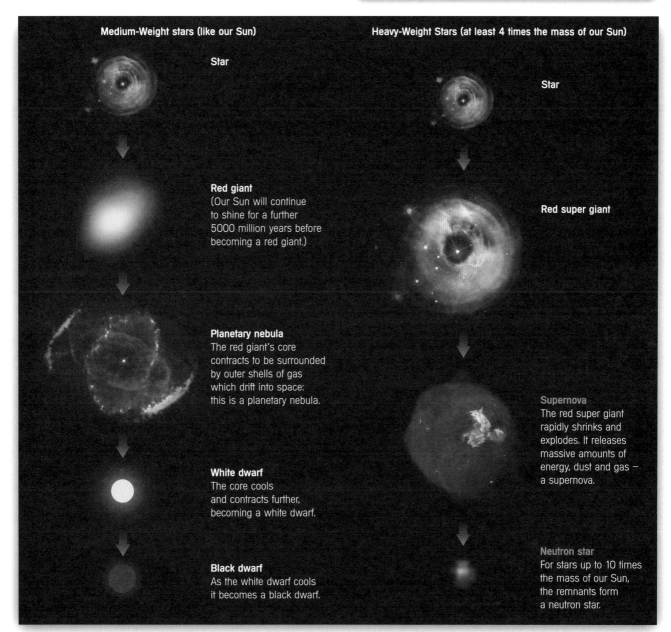

Medium-Weight stars (like our Sun)

Star

Red giant
(Our Sun will continue to shine for a further 5000 million years before becoming a red giant.)

Planetary nebula
The red giant's core contracts to be surrounded by outer shells of gas which drift into space: this is a planetary nebula.

White dwarf
The core cools and contracts further, becoming a white dwarf.

Black dwarf
As the white dwarf cools it becomes a black dwarf.

Heavy-Weight Stars (at least 4 times the mass of our Sun)

Star

Red super giant

Supernova
The red super giant rapidly shrinks and explodes. It releases massive amounts of energy, dust and gas – a supernova.

Neutron star
For stars up to 10 times the mass of our Sun, the remnants form a neutron star.

The Earth in the Universe

Other Galaxies

If a source of light is **moving away** from us, the wavelengths of light are **longer** than if the source is stationary.

Wavelengths of light from nearby galaxies are longer than scientists expect. This means the galaxies are **moving away** from us.

(HT) Observations made by **Edwin Hubble** showed that almost all galaxies are moving away from us and the further away they are, the faster they are moving away. He developed this into **Hubble's Law** which states:

The speed at which a galaxy is moving away is proportional to its distance.

If all the galaxies are moving away from us, this must mean that space is **expanding**.

The Beginning and The End

The **Big Bang** theory says that the Universe began with a huge explosion 14 000 million years ago.

The future of the universe depends on its amount of mass. Measuring the amount of mass is difficult so its fate is hard to predict. If there **isn't enough** mass the Universe will keep **expanding**.

If there's **too much** mass, gravity will pull everything back together and the Universe will **collapse**.

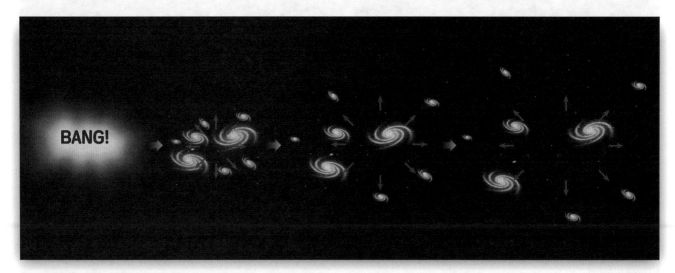

BANG!

Aliens

In 1996, a Mars meteorite appeared to contain an **ancient alien fossil**. Different explanations were offered but the debate still rages on.

If there are other life forms they are likely to be on other planets or moons. Astronomers have detected some stars with orbiting planets.

There's no confirmed evidence of alien life. Many scientists think that with the vast numbers of stars and galaxies, it's unlikely that only Earth has life.

Key Words

Big Bang • **Hubble's Law**

What Killed the Dinosaurs?

Evidence shows that dinosaurs became extinct around 65 million years ago. One explanation is that an **asteroid** hit Earth.

The Facts:
- Fossils show that dinosaurs gradually died out.
- The chances of a large asteroid hitting Earth are very small.
- If an asteroid did hit Earth, everything in the **impact zone** would be destroyed.
- Large asteroids have hit Earth in the past. The Chicxulub crater in Mexico provides evidence of this. Scientists estimate the energy of this asteroid on impact was **10 000 times greater** than all the world's nuclear weapons combined.
- A layer of **iridium** (a metallic element common in asteroids) is found all over Earth.

The Explanations:
- The layer of iridium could be the result of an **asteroid collision**.
- A big asteroid would have caused **firestorms**, **shock waves** and possibly climate change. Dinosaurs couldn't have survived.
- The collision could have **released sulfur** and caused **strong acid rain** for weeks.
- Dust could have blocked the Sun and caused plants to die, affecting the whole food chain.

Scientific Explanation

A good **scientific explanation** will provide reasons for **all** of the data. Many explain some facts, but not all of them.

Facts and explanations could be used to evaluate whether an asteroid could destroy the human race.

Unlike the dinosaurs, humans have the technology to detect asteroids, but that doesn't mean we would be able to stop it, or survive an impact.

Module P1 Summary

The Earth

Evidence in rocks show us how the Earth has changed through:

- **erosion**
- **craters** being made
- **mountains forming**.

The Earth must be **older** than its **oldest rocks**.

(HT) The **oldest rocks** on Earth are about **4000 million years old**.

The **Earth** is made up of…

- the crust
- mantle
- core.

Continental Drift

Wegener's continental drift theory = the continents **fit together** and fossils, rock patterns and mountain ranges **match up**.

Wegener's theory was **rejected** by his peers at the time ⟹ Evidence from **seafloor spreading** led to it becoming **accepted**.

Tectonic Plates and Seafloor Spreading

Earth's crust is divided into **tectonic plates**; these meet at **plate boundaries**.

Tectonic plates…

- **float** on the **mantle**
- **move apart, towards** or **past** each other.

The **mantle** is **fairly solid** below the crust; further down it is **liquid**.

Convection currents in the mantle cause the plates to move; **magma** can rise to the surface and harden, forming new **seafloor**.

(HT) Plate Tectonics

Earth's **magnetic field** changes polarity every million years and produces **rock stripes** of **alternating polarity**. These occur at **constructive plate boundaries**.

Subduction = the denser **oceanic plate** is forced under the **continental plate**. Occurs at **destructive plate boundaries**.

Mountain ranges form along **colliding** plate boundaries as **sedimentary rock** is forced up by a **collision**.

Plate movement is crucial in the **rock cycle**.

Geohazards

Geohazards...
- are **natural hazards** (e.g. floods)
- can strike without warning so authorities take **precautionary measures**.

The Universe

The **Big Bang** theory explains how the Universe began.

(HT) The **Solar System** formed 5000 million years ago.

The Solar System began as **dust** and **gas** clouds ➡ **Nuclear fusion** formed the Sun ➡ Smaller masses like **planets**, **moons**, **asteroids** and **comets** formed around the Sun.

The Sun's energy comes from **nuclear fusion**: hydrogen atoms **fuse together**.

(HT) The **nuclei** of hydrogen atoms fuse together during nuclear fusion.

Other galaxies are **moving away** from us.

(HT) **Hubble's Law** = the speed at which a galaxy is moving away is proportional to its distance.

Space and the Stars

If the distance is great enough, **light speed** can be measured.

(HT) **Speed of light** = 300 000km/s.

Vast space distances are measured in **light years**.

The distance of a star can be measured using **relative brightness** or **parallax**.

Stars produce radiation.

Stars have a **finite life** and eventually become **red giants** or **red super giants**.

Scientific Explanations

There's no proof of **alien life**, although many scientists think it's possible.

One theory for the extinction of the dinosaurs is that an **asteroid** hit Earth.

A good scientific explanation will provide reasons for **all** the data.

Facts and **explanations** can be used to **evaluate** a theory. A theory needs evaluating by **other scientists** before it's **accepted** – the **Peer review** process.

Module P1 Practice Questions

1 The drawing shows the structure of the Earth. Match
statements **A, B, C** and **D** with the labels **1–4**
on the drawing. Enter the appropriate number in the
boxes provided.

A Inner core ⬭

B Outer core ⬭

C Mantle ⬭

D Crust ⬭

2 Wegener was a scientist who proposed the theory of continental drift. What evidence did Wegener use
to support his theory? Tick the three correct options.

A The jigsaw fit of some continents. ⬭

B Other people believed him. ⬭

C Rock patterns are the same on different continents. ⬭

D He used the periodic table. ⬭

E Fossil remains. ⬭

3 **a)** Fill in the missing word to complete the sentence below:

Earth's crust is divided into _____ plates.

b) Name the three ways these plates can move.

i) _____

ii) _____

iii) _____

4 **a)** Circle the correct options in the following sentence:

Convection / combustion / magma / mantle currents in the **convection / combustion / magma / mantle**

cause **convection / combustion / magma / mantle** to rise and form new oceanic crust.

b) What is this theory known as?

_____

(HT) **5** How old is the Solar System?

_____

6 Fill in the missing words to complete the sentences below:

a) The Solar System began when _____ and _____ clouds were

pulled together by _____ which created intense _____ .

b) _____ fusion began and the Sun was born.

c) Smaller masses also formed, which _____ the Sun.

7 Name two smaller masses in the Solar System.

a) _____ **b)** _____

8 What are vast distances in space measured in?

_____

9 What two ways can the distance of a star be measured?

a) _____ **b)** _____

10 Medium-weight stars like the Sun eventually become a red giant. Fill in the missing words below to complete the next three stages of its life cycle.

a) The red giant's core contracts and it becomes a planetary _____ .

b) The star's core cools and contracts further, becoming a _____ dwarf.

c) It cools further to become a _____ dwarf.

11 Fill in the missing words to complete the sentence below:

If a source of light is moving away from us, the _____ of light are

_____ than if the source was stationary.

12 Name a theory of how the Universe began.

_____

Keeping Healthy

Infection

Infections are caused by harmful microorganisms:

- **Bacteria**, e.g. bubonic plague, TB and cystitis. Treated by antibiotics.
- **Fungi**, e.g. athlete's foot, thrush and ringworm. Treated by anti-fungal medicine and antibiotics.
- **Viruses**, e.g. Asian bird flu, common cold, HIV, measles and smallpox. Very difficult to treat.

The Body's Defence System

Microorganisms can be found on any surface and in the air we breathe.

The human body has a defence system of **physical** and **chemical** barriers which stop you getting ill:

- **Skin** forms a physical barrier.
- Chemicals in **sweat** and **tears**, and **hydrochloric acid** in the stomach, kill microorganisms.

The body provides ideal conditions for microorganisms to grow; it's **warm** with plenty of **nutrients** and **moisture**. Once in your body, harmful microorganisms reproduce very rapidly.

Symptoms of an illness only show when there's a significant amount of infection. The symptoms are caused by microorganisms damaging infected cells, e.g. bursting or producing harmful toxins.

The Immune Response

If microorganisms get into your body, the **immune system** is activated. Two types of **white blood cells** play a major role in this response.

One type of white blood cell is activated when you cut yourself:

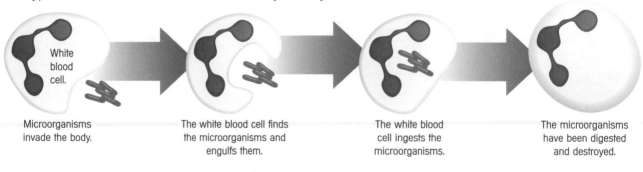

White blood cell.			
Microorganisms invade the body.	The white blood cell finds the microorganisms and engulfs them.	The white blood cell ingests the microorganisms.	The microorganisms have been digested and destroyed.

Another type of white blood cell makes **antibodies**:

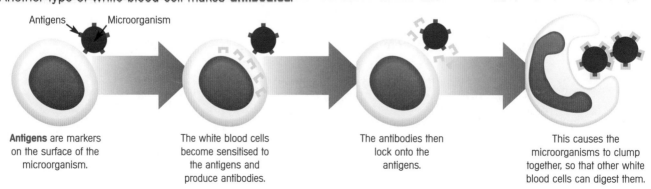

Antigens   Microorganism

Antigens are markers on the surface of the microorganism.	The white blood cells become sensitised to the antigens and produce antibodies.	The antibodies then lock onto the antigens.	This causes the microorganisms to clump together, so that other white blood cells can digest them.

Specialisation of Antibodies

Different microorganisms cause different diseases. Microorganisms have **unique markers**, called **antigens**, on their surface. White blood cells produce antibodies specific to the marker they need to attack.

White blood cells 'remember' the antigens after infection and can produce antibodies quicker if the microorganism appears again. This is **natural immunity**.

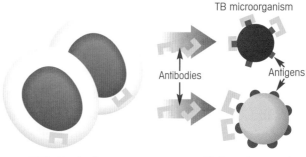

Example – antibodies to fight TB will not fight cholera.

TB microorganism
Antibodies
Antigens
White blood cells
Cholera microorganism

Vaccination

A **vaccination** helps the body develop **immunity** and produce **specific** antibodies so microorganisms can be destroyed before they cause **infection**.

Vaccinations are never completely safe and can produce **side effects**. Most side effects are minor, e.g. mild fever or rash, but some people are affected more than others.

Extreme side effects like encephalitis (inflammation of the brain) are **rare**. The MMR vaccine has a 1 in 1 000 000 chance of encephalitis, but the risk of getting it from measles itself is much higher.

1 A weakened/dead strain of the microorganism is injected. Antigens on the modified microorganism's surface cause the white blood cells to produce specific antibodies.

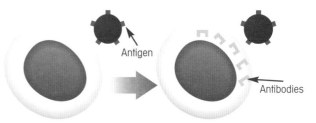

Antigen
Antibodies

2 The white blood cells that are capable of quickly producing the specific antibody remain in the bloodstream.

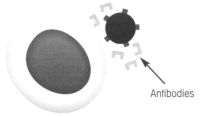

Antibodies

Mutating Viruses

Some vaccines have to be redeveloped regularly because viruses can **mutate** (change) to produce **new strains**. For example, flu vaccinations are **renewed every year** because new strains appear.

Key Words

Antibody • Antigen • Bacteria • Fungi • Immune system • Mutate • Natural immunity • Side effect • Virus

HT **HIV** (Human Immunodeficiency Virus) attacks the **immune system** and can lead to **AIDS** (Acquired Immune Deficiency Syndrome).

Infected people can die from illnesses like the common cold. HIV can be carried for years without being detected and can be passed on.

HIV is difficult to make a vaccine for. It **infects** the **white blood cells** that normally fight viruses. HIV can **mutate rapidly** and produce new strains.

Keeping Healthy

Choices

People can refuse to have a vaccination. But the more who say no, the greater the chance of a **disease outbreak** (epidemic) and the **faster** it will spread.

(HT) It's important to vaccinate as many people as possible to prevent epidemics like measles. If **more** than 95% of the population are vaccinated then the unvaccinated will be protected too, as the risk of contact with an infected person is **small**. If the percentage drops **below** 95% then there's a greater chance of contact with infected people.

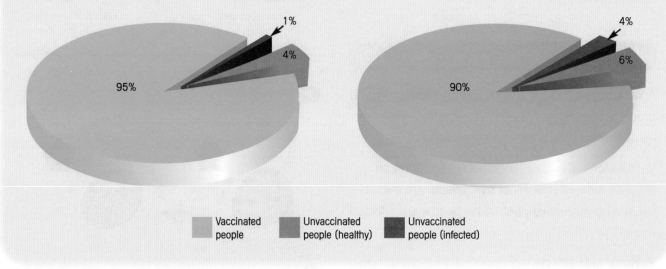

| ■ Vaccinated people | ■ Unvaccinated people (healthy) | ■ Unvaccinated people (infected) |

Vaccination Policy

Health authorities have to develop a policy for each vaccination to **benefit the majority**. People hold different views so there will always be those who disagree.

(HT) The following **key factors** should be considered:
- How **high** is the **risk** of infection? Is the disease common in the UK?
- Who is **most at risk** e.g. the young, the elderly?
- Is the vaccination **safe**? Has it been tested for side effects?
- What is the **cost**? Can the Government afford to give free vaccines?

There's a difference between what **can** be done and what **should** be done.

For example, the government might have the ability to vaccinate everyone, but it can't force people to have a vaccination. People may refuse to have a vaccination for different reasons:
- It may conflict with religious / personal **beliefs**.
- Society gives us the right to **choose**.
- Some people may be more prone to side effects.

Different courses of action may be taken in different social and environmental contexts.

Antibiotics

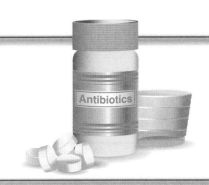

Antibiotics are chemicals (drugs):
- They can kill **bacteria** and **fungi**.
- They can't kill **viruses** (so aren't prescribed for colds).

Resistance to Antibiotics

Over time, bacteria and fungi can become **resistant** to antibiotics.

> **HT** **Random mutations** can occur in the genes of microorganisms:
> - **New strains** develop.
> - These are less affected by antibiotics so they can **reproduce** and **pass on** their resistance.

As varieties of bacteria and fungi become resistant, there are **fewer ways** to defeat them.

There's growing concern that microorganisms which are resistant to all drugs will develop (i.e. superbugs). In the UK, diseases such as MRSA (Methicillin Resistant Staphylococcus aureus) have a high degree of drug resistance.

To help prevent antibiotic resistance…
- doctors should only prescribe them when **completely necessary**
- patients should always **complete the course**.

The Effect of Antibiotics on Infection

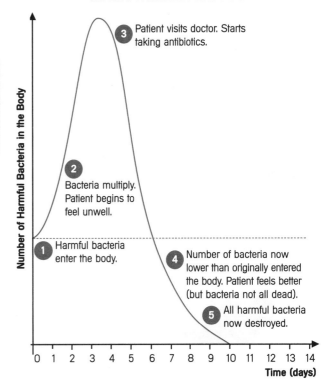

Key Words

Antibiotic • Bacteria • Fungi • Virus

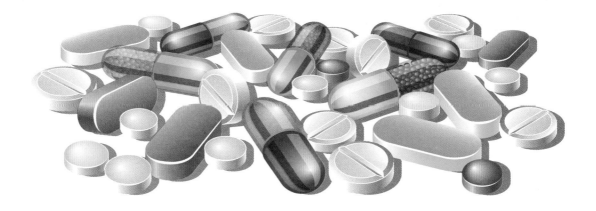

Keeping Healthy

Testing New Drugs

New drugs are tested for **safety** and **effectiveness** before they can be used. The methods used are often controversial.

Tests on Human Cells grown in the Laboratory	Tests on Animals
Advantages • Shows if drugs are effective. • Shows if drugs will damage cells. • No people or animals are harmed.	**Advantages** • Shows if drugs are effective within body conditions. • Shows if drugs are safe for whole body.
Disadvantages • Doesn't show effects on whole organism. • Some say growing human cells is wrong.	**Disadvantages** • Animals can suffer and die. • Animals may react differently to humans.

Clinical Trials

Clinical trials are carried out on…
- **healthy volunteers** to test for safety
- people with the illness to test for safety and effectiveness.

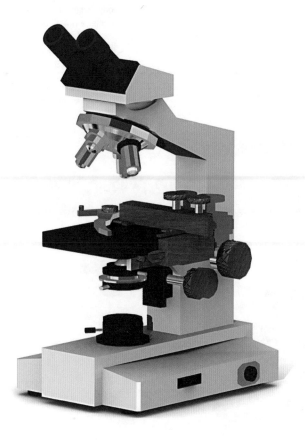

HT Clinical trials compare the effects of **new** and **old** drugs.

Blind trials – Patients **don't know** which drugs they're given but the doctor **does**. If the patient knows, they may give biased information. It's possible the doctor's body language may give clues.

Double-blind trials – Neither patient nor doctor know which drug is used. Results should be very accurate, due to removing bias. Sometimes it's impossible to keep what the drug is from the doctor, e.g. if the patient says the new drug has a different taste.

Placebos (dummy drugs) are occasionally used but create an ethical dilemma. They give **false hope**; the patient hopes the pill cures them, but the doctor knows it will not.

It's difficult to hide which patient is taking a placebo as a new drug may have certain obvious side effects, e.g. increased urine production. So, the patient and doctor would know if the patient had been given a placebo.

The Heart

The heart…
- pumps blood around the body in order to provide cells with **oxygen** and **nutrients**, and take away **waste**
- is made up of **muscle cells**, so it needs a blood supply to **function** properly.

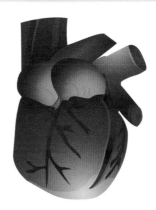

Arteries and Veins

The main blood vessels are **arteries** and **veins**. Their structure is related to their function.

Arteries carry blood away from the heart **towards** the organs. Substances from the blood can't pass through artery walls.

Veins carry blood from the organs **back** to the heart. Substances can't pass through the veins' walls.

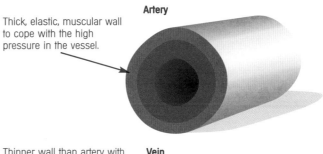

Artery

Thick, elastic, muscular wall to cope with the high pressure in the vessel.

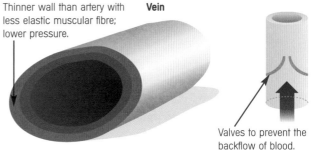

Thinner wall than artery with less elastic muscular fibre; lower pressure.

Vein

Valves to prevent the backflow of blood.

Heart Disease

Heart disease…
- is a **structural** or **functional** abnormality which can lead to heart attack
- is usually caused by **lifestyle** and/or **genetic** factors. It's **not** caused by infection.

Lifestyle factors that can lead to heart disease include excessive alcohol, poor diet, smoking and stress.

A heart attack occurs when **fatty deposits** build up in blood vessels supplying the heart. Blood flow is restricted and muscle cells don't get enough oxygen and nutrients.

Heart disease is more common in the UK than in non-industrialised countries.

Precautions people can take include…
- regular exercise, e.g. 20 minutes brisk walking every day
- not smoking
- maintaining a healthy weight and reducing salt intake.

Key Words

Artery • Clinical trial • Placebo • Vein

Keeping Healthy

Epidemiological Studies

Epidemiological studies help identify **lifestyle factors** that lead to heart disease. These studies examine the **incidence** (number of cases) and **distribution** of heart disease in large populations.

Correlation

Scientists look at a large **cross-section** of cases to see if there's a **correlation** (link) between a factor and an outcome. For example, there is a correlation between a **high-fat diet** (factor) and **heart attacks** (outcome).

A large proportion of people who suffered heart attacks had a high-fat diet. But, not all people with a fatty diet had a heart attack. This suggests a fatty diet increases the chances of a heart attack, but doesn't always lead to one.

HT A correlation doesn't necessarily mean that the factor is a cause.

For example, a study could uncover a correlation between the number of kilograms someone is overweight and the amount of diet cola they consume. This doesn't mean diet cola causes obesity. In fact, they might drink diet cola because they're overweight.

Samples

Scientists look at a large sample of cases to see what is **typical** and what is **atypical** (unusual).

An individual case might be atypical. For example, someone who's smoked most of their life might live to 98 without getting lung cancer. If you looked at

this case alone, you may think this proves that smoking helps you live longer!

To ensure a **fair test**, samples should be closely matched (e.g. similar diet and alcohol intake) so that only the factor being investigated varies.

HT Data can be used to argue whether or not a factor increases the chance of an outcome and to make predictions.

For example, the graph shows there's a negative correlation between the number of alcoholic drinks consumed and a person's dexterity (ability to move hands easily). As X increases, Y decreases. This means that given a value for X, it's possible to make a prediction of the value of Y.

Even if data supports a correlation, scientists may still reject it. It's only likely to be accepted if they can find a **plausible** (likely) explanation for how that factor can bring about the outcome.

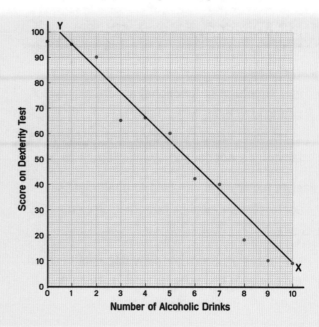

The Peer Review Process

Scientists follow procedures when conducting research like epidemiological studies to ensure their findings are reliable:

1. **Epidemiological study** – the scientist may discover a correlation and makes a **hypothesis**, e.g. that factor X increases the chance of outcome Y.
2. **Further investigation** – they conduct further experiments to gather data to test the hypothesis.
3. **Report findings** – the scientist writes a paper detailing the hypothesis, how the experiment was carried out, the results, and the conclusion (whether the data supports the hypothesis).
4. **Peer review** – peers (other scientists who work in that field) check the findings for faults and may repeat the experiments.
5. **Findings released** – if it's decided the research was correct and the conclusions are accurate, the findings are published or presented.
6. **Feedback** – all scientists can then **evaluate** it. It may lead to **further advances** or could be **challenged** – someone may see a new problem.

Reliability and Accuracy

The **peer review** process is very important. The more scientists that **evaluate** the findings, the more likely it is that **errors** or problems will be spotted, and the more **reliable** the results may be.

Sometimes preliminary results that haven't been fully reviewed by other scientists are leaked. These aren't reliable and may turn out to be inaccurate or wrong. Inaccurate information can cause problems, e.g. it can cause false hope or panic.

HT Unfortunately, a small minority of scientists make claims that **aren't true**. They might do this to improve their reputation or for funding.

If a new claim is reliable, other scientists should get the same results. If this isn't possible, the claim will not be trusted. Likewise, if a scientist refuses to show evidence (e.g. details of experiments and data), their findings must be taken as being **unreliable**.

Key Words

Epidemiological study • Peer review

Module B2 Summary

The Body's Defence System

Infections are caused by...
- **bacteria**
- **fungi**
- **viruses**.

The human body has a **defence system** of **physical** and **chemical barriers**.

Symptoms of an illness only show when there's a **significant** amount of infection.

Two types of **white blood cell** are part of the **immune system's response**:
- One type **engulfs** and **digests** microorganisms.
- Another type makes **antibodies**.

Antigens = unique markers on microorganisms.
White blood cells remember antigens to produce antibodies quicker.

Vaccination

Vaccination...
- helps the body develop **immunity** and produce **specific antibodies**
- can have **side effects**.

Some vaccines need to be developed regularly because viruses can **mutate**.

(HT) **HIV**...
- is difficult to make a vaccine for
- infects the white blood cells.

People can choose not to have a vaccination.

It's important to vaccinate as many people as possible to prevent **epidemics** and **reduce the risk** of becoming infected. **Health authorities** develop **policies** to benefit the **majority**.

(HT) The government may have the ability to vaccinate everyone, but it can't force people.

Different courses of action may be taken in different social and environmental contexts.

Antibiotics

Antibiotics are **chemicals** which kill **bacteria** and **fungi**. They **can't** kill **viruses**.

Bacteria and fungi can become **resistant** to antibiotics.

(HT) **Random gene mutations** occur in the microorganism ⟹ **New strains** develop ⟹ These are less affected by the drug and pass this resistance on.

Doctors should only prescribe antibiotics when **completely necessary**. Patients should **always complete the course**.

Testing New Drugs

New drugs are tested for **safety** and **effectiveness**. Methods can be controversial (e.g. testing on animals).

Clinical trials are carried out on healthy volunteers and people with the illness.

HT Clinical trials compare the effects of new and old drugs:
- **Blind Trials.**
- **Double-Blind Trials.**

Dummy drugs called **placebos** can be used. These can give false hope so create an ethical dilemma.

The Heart, Arteries and Veins

The **heart**…
- pumps blood to provide cells with **oxygen** and **nutrients** and take away **waste**
- is made up of muscle cells.

The main blood vessels are…
- **arteries**
- **veins**.

Heart disease is…
- a **structural** or **functional** abnormality which can lead to heart attack
- is usually caused by **lifestyle** (e.g. diet) and / or **genetic factors**.

Scientific Studies

Scientists look at a **large sample** to look for a **correlation** between a **factor** and an **outcome**.

Samples are closely matched to ensure a **fair test**.

HT A correlation doesn't always mean that the factor is a cause.

Data can be used to argue whether or not a factor increases the chance of an outcome and make predictions.

Peer Reviews

Peer Review process = other scientists check the results for errors to make sure the results are reliable.

HT A minority of scientists make claims that **aren't true**.

Findings must be taken as **unreliable** if a scientist **refuses** to show their evidence.

1 Name the three groups of disease-causing microorganisms.

a) _____ b) _____ c) _____

2 Bacteria can grow very rapidly. They can only do so if the correct conditions are present. Circle the three best factors for bacterial growth.

Warmth   **Safety**   **Humidity**   **Food**   **Attractiveness**

3 The body has a number of physical and chemical barriers to infection by microorganisms. Fill in the labels on the diagram below to show these barriers.

a) _____

b) _____

c) _____

d) _____

4 **A**, **B**, **C** and **D** describe the four stages that take place when white blood cells attack a foreign microorganism. Put them in the correct order using numbers **1–4**.

A Microorganisms are ingested by the white blood cell.   ◯

B Microorganisms are detected by the body.   ◯

C Microorganisms are completely digested and destroyed.   ◯

D White blood cell surrounds the microorganism.   ◯

5 Label the diagram below which shows how the body fights infection.

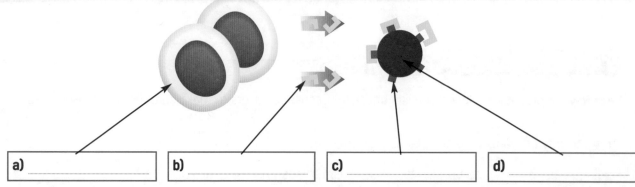

a) _____   b) _____   c) _____   d) _____

6 Vaccines prevent disease. What is contained in a vaccine? Tick the correct option.

A   Antibiotics ◯

B   A weakened or dead strain of the disease-causing microorganism ◯

C   An active strain of the disease-causing microorganism ◯

D   Antibodies ◯

7 a) Why can't vaccines ever be completely safe?

....

b) Why do new vaccines have to be developed regularly for diseases such as Flu?

....

HT **8** Which of the following statements about HIV are true? Tick the three correct options.

A   HIV mutates at a high rate in the body. ◯

B   HIV mutates at a slow rate in the body. ◯

C   HIV attacks the immune system. ◯

D   New HIV strains are unaffected by a vaccine. ◯

E   Vaccines destroy new HIV strains. ◯

F   HIV improves the immune system. ◯

9 Why is it important to finish a course of antibiotics?

....

....

10 Fill in the missing words to complete the sentences below:

The main blood vessels are .... and .... Heart attacks occur

when .... deposits build up in .... supplying the heart.

11 Scientists carry out research following certain procedures. Place the numbers **1–6** in the boxes to put
the following stages in the correct order.

A   Peer Review. ◯   B   Report Findings. ◯

C   Epidemiological Study. ◯   D   Feedback. ◯

E   Further Investigation. ◯   F   Release findings. ◯

Material Choices

Natural and Synthetic Materials

Materials are chemicals, or mixtures of chemicals. Some materials come from **living things** e.g. cotton and paper (plants), silk and wool (animals).

Synthetic materials, produced by **chemical synthesis**, can be made as **alternatives**. For example, the petrochemical industry refines **crude oil** to produce fuels, lubricants and raw materials for chemical synthesis. Only a small proportion of crude oil is used in chemical synthesis.

to natural polymers

Crude oil, when extracted, contains **mainly hydrocarbons**, which are **chain molecules** containing only hydrogen and carbon atoms. This means that crude oil can be separated by **fractional distillation** into different parts, or fractions (groups of hydrocarbons of similar lengths).

Hydrocarbons have **different boiling points** as their molecular chains are **different lengths**.

Properties of Materials

Different solid materials have different properties, For example, they…

*   have different **melting points** and **densities**
*   can be strong or weak, rigid or flexible, hard or soft
*   will be better suited to some uses.

Properties of the materials used will affect the **durability** and **effectiveness** of an end product, so manufacturers test and assess the material carefully beforehand.

Material	Properties	Uses
Unvulcanised rubbers	• Low tensile strength • Soft and flexible/elastic	• Erasers • Rubber bands
Vulcanised rubbers	• High tensile strength • Hard and flexible/elastic	• Car tyres • Conveyor belts • Shock absorbers
Plastic – polythene	• Lightweight (low density) • Flexible and easily moulded	• Plastic bags • Moulded containers
Plastic – polystyrene	• Lightweight (low density) • Stiff • Good thermal insulator as foam • Water resistant	• Meat trays • Egg cartons • Coffee cups • Protecting appliances and electronics
Synthetic fibres – nylon	• Lightweight (low density) • Tough and waterproof • Blocks ultraviolet light	• Clothing • Climbing ropes
Synthetic fibres – polyester	• Lightweight (low density) • Tough and waterproof	• Clothing • Bottles

Polymerisation

Polymerisation is an important chemical process in which small hydrocarbon molecules (**monomers**) are joined together to make very long molecules (**polymers**).

For example the long-chain molecule polymer **poly(ethene)**, often called **polythene**, is made from ethene monomers:

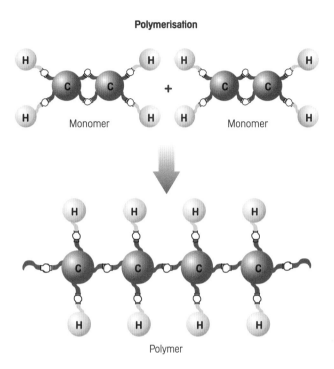

Polymerisation

Monomer   +   Monomer

Polymer

```
  H      H H      H              H   H   H   H
   \    / | \    /               |   |   |   |
    C=C  +  C=C  + many more  → – C – C – C – C –
   /    \ | /    \               |   |   |   |
  H      H H      H              H   H   H   H

   Ethene Monomer              Polythene Polymer
```

During a chemical reaction the number of atoms of each element in the products must be the same as in the reactants.

Using Polymerisation

Polymerisation can be used to create a **wide range** of **different materials**, which have **different properties** so can be used for **different purposes**.

Many traditional (natural) materials have been **replaced** by polymers because of their **superior properties**.

For example, carrier bags used to be made of **paper**. Now they are made from **polythene** because it's **stronger** and **waterproof**.

Window frames were made of **wood** but are now often made of **polychloroethene** because it's <u>unreactive</u> and **doesn't rot**.

to what?

Key Words

Chemical synthesis • Crude oil • Fractional distillation • Hydrocarbon • Monomer • Polymer • Polymerisation

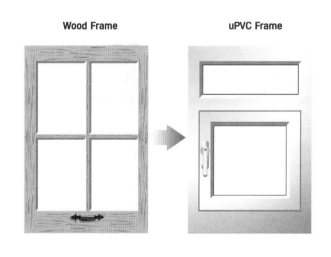

Wood Frame   uPVC Frame

Paper Bags   Plastic Bags

Material Choices

Molecular Structure of Materials

Properties of solid materials depend on how their **particles** are arranged and held together.

Natural rubber is a mass of **long-chain molecules**. Atoms are held together by strong covalent bonds, but there are **very weak forces** between the molecules. They can slide over one another and the material can stretch. Natural rubber…

- is very **flexible**
- has a **low** melting point as little energy is needed to separate molecules.

Vulcanised rubber is a mass of tangled molecules where the atoms are held together by strong covalent bonds. The molecules also have **crosslinks** which are strong covalent bonds between the long-chain molecules. Vulcanised rubber…

- is quite **rigid** and **hard** to stretch as the molecules will not slide over each other
- needs lots of energy to separate molecules and has a **high** melting temperature.

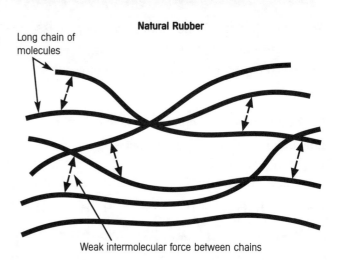

Natural Rubber

Long chain of molecules

Weak intermolecular force between chains

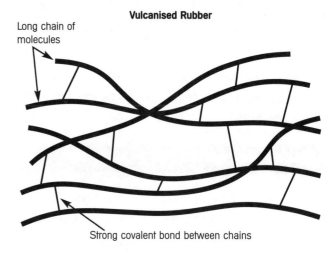

Vulcanised Rubber

Long chain of molecules

Strong covalent bond between chains

Modifications in Polymers

Modifications can produce changes to the properties of **polymers**.

Increasing the chain length means that there is more contact and more forces between the molecules, which makes them stronger.

Crosslinks are formed by atoms **bonding** between polymer molecules, so they can no longer move. This makes a **harder** material.

An example of crosslinking is **vulcanisation**, when sulfur atoms form crosslinks between rubber molecules. Vulcanised rubber is used to make car tyres and conveyor belts.

Adding **plasticizers** makes a polymer **softer** and **more flexible**. A plasticizer is a small molecule that sits between molecules and forces the chains apart. This means the forces between the chains are **weaker** so molecules can move more **easily**. **Plasticized PVC** is used in children's toys, and **un-plasticized PVC** (uPVC) in window frames.

(HT) A polymer can also be modified by packing molecules more **closely** together to form a **crystalline** polymer.

Intermolecular forces are slightly stronger so the polymer is **stronger, denser** and has a slightly **higher** melting point.

Life Cycle of a Product

New products must undergo a **Life Cycle Assessment** (LCA) which has three phases:

- **Manufacture**
- **Use**
- **Disposal**.

Each part of the life cycle is assessed for its **environmental impact** by the amount of **energy** and **materials** that will be used, and how materials will be **obtained** and **disposed** of.

(HT) The LCA outcome is dependent on several factors, including the use of the end product.

LCAs encourage companies to reduce waste and be aware of the impact they have on the environment. Laws were introduced, including cash incentives to encourage **recycling** and a tax to discourage **landfill** sites.

The purpose of an LCA is to help find the most **sustainable** method so that current needs are met without damaging resources for the future.

Factors to be Assessed in an LCA

Manufacture - Resources and energy to make the product. The environmental impact of making the product from the material.

Use - Energy needed to use the product, e.g. electricity. Energy and chemicals needed to maintain the product. Environmental impact.

Disposal - Energy needed to dispose of the product. Environmental impact of landfill, incineration and recycling.

Materials

Different materials can perform the **same** job.

For example, disposable nappies are more convenient but an LCA shows that re-usable nappies are environmentally better. Evidence in the table shows that re-using nappies uses less resources and produces less waste.

Impact per Baby, per Year	Re-usable Nappies	Disposable Nappies
Energy needed to produce product	2532MJ	8900MJ
Waste water	12.4m³	28m³
Raw materials used	29kg	569kg
Domestic solid waste produced	4kg	361kg

Functions

The **same** material can be used to perform **different** jobs. For example, Teflon® is used in atomic bombs and non-stick saucepans.

Key Words

Crystalline • Polymer • Life Cycle Assessment • Plasticizer • Sustainable

Material Choices

Waste Management

There are three methods of **waste disposal**: use of **landfill** sites, **incineration** and **recycling**.

Use of Landfill Sites

Materials such as plastics are **non-biodegradable**. Microorganisms **can't** decompose them. Some materials that degrade produce **methane**, a **landfill** gas. Too much methane can cause explosions.

If landfill sites are properly lined, they cause no harm and eventually land can be reclaimed, e.g. for parks. However, **toxic waste** has escaped when sites have been poorly engineered.

Incineration

Incinerating materials produces **air pollution** and wastes valuable resources. Some plastics produce **toxic gases** when burned, e.g. PVC produces hydrogen chloride gas.

Newer incinerators burn at high temperatures to avoid producing many harmful gases. Heat from an incinerator can be used to produce **steam** to drive a generator and save on **fossil fuels**. Apart from any gases, the only other waste will be **ash**.

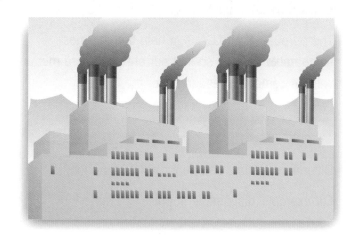

Recycling

Recycling conserves raw materials, money and energy. People should **re-use** products such as carrier bags and glass bottles.

But there are disadvantages with recycling. It's **expensive** and **time-consuming** to recycle some materials, e.g. plastics need to be sorted into types.

Every time polythene is recycled its long molecules tend to **tear**. It becomes **weaker** and the quality is **reduced**.

Example – A Polypropylene Food Box

Stage of Life Cycle	Energy Requirements Assessment Questions	Environmental Impact Assessment Questions
Manufacture	How much energy would be needed… • to drill and distil the oil? • for polymerisation? • to mould the box? • to transport the materials between stages?	• How much oil will be taken from natural reserves? • What's the risk of spillage during transportation? • What pollutants and waste materials are produced during manufacture and transportation?
Use	How much energy would be required… • to fill the boxes with food? • to store the boxes, e.g. in a fridge? • to transport them?	• How will the product be transported between factory, shop and home? • What pollutants and waste materials are produced during filling and transportation?
Disposal	How much energy would be used or recovered if the box was… • re-used or recycled? • incinerated? • thrown away?	• Would incineration produce pollutants / toxic gases? • What is the value of materials and energy wasted if the box is thrown away? • How much landfill would it generate?

The government makes laws but manufacturers must make choices. They must **evaluate** their answers and **compare** LCAs for using different materials.

In some cases the most environmentally friendly method may be too expensive.

The assessment questions can be answered using **scientific models** and **investigations**. But, some answers can't be found this way.

For example, the manufacturer needs to decide whether the amounts of energy and resources used, and the environmental impact, are justified.

Key Words

Incineration • Landfill • Non-biodegradable • Recycling

Module C2 Summary

Natural and Synthetic Materials

Materials are **chemicals**.

Some materials come from **living things** and some are **synthetic** (made by **chemical synthesis**).

Crude oil…

* contains mainly **hydrocarbons** (**chain molecules** containing **hydrogen** and **carbon** atoms)
* can be separated by **fractional distillation**
* is refined for **chemical synthesis.**

Hydrocarbons have **different boiling points** because their molecular chains are **different lengths** and have different forces between them.

Properties of Materials

Different solid materials have **different properties**, e.g.…

* **melting point**
* **densities**
* **strength**
* **rigidity**.

Different materials are better suited to some uses.

Properties of a material affect a product's **durability** and **effectiveness**.

Polymerisation

Polymerisation = **monomers** join together to form **polymers**.

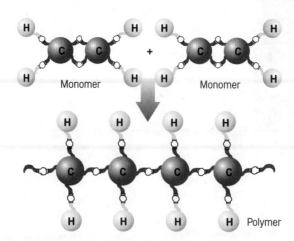

The number of elements in the **products** must be the same as the **reactants**.

Polymerisation can create **different materials** with **different properties**.

Many traditional materials have been **replaced** ➡ Polymers have **superior properties**.

Modifications in Polymers

Properties of a material depend on how **particles** are **arranged** and **held together**.

Modifications can produce changes to the properties of polymers by...
*   **increasing** the chain length
*   forming **crosslinks** (atoms bond between polymers)
*   adding **plasticizers** (small molecules that force the chains apart).

HT **Crystalline polymer** = molecules packed more closely together ➡ Forces are stronger so the polymer is stronger.

Life Cycle of a Product

Life Cycle Assessment (LCA) has three phases:
*   Manufacture
*   Use
*   Disposal.

The LCA assesses each phase for...
*   **environmental impact**
*   the amount of **energy** and **materials used**
*   how materials will be **obtained** and **disposed of**.

An LCA can help find the best material for the job.

HT The LCA outcome depends on several factors, including the **use** of the **end product**.

LCAs encourage companies to...
*   **reduce waste**
*   be aware of **impact on the environment**.

An LCA's purpose = find the most **sustainable method**.

Manufacturers must make **choices**, **evaluate** their answers and **compare LCAs** for using different materials in a product.

The LCA questions can be answered using **scientific models** and **investigations**.

Waste Management

The three main methods of disposal:
*   **Landfill sites** (some waste can't decompose).
*   **Incineration** (produces air pollution).
*   **Recycling** (conserves raw materials).

Module C2 Practice Questions

1 Name two natural materials that can be used to make clothing.

a) .... **b)** ....

2 Fill in the missing words to complete the sentences below:

a) Natural materials are extracted from .... and ....

whereas synthetic materials are manufactured from simple ....

b) Crude oil is mainly made up of ....

c) A small proportion of crude oil is used in chemical ....

3 What properties would be important in the manufacture of car tyres? Tick the three correct options.

A Hard ⬭ **B** Absorbent ⬭

C Lightweight ⬭ **D** Insulating ⬭

E Flexible ⬭ **F** Strong ⬭

4 Expanded polystyrene is used in lifejackets for canoeists. What two main properties are important for this use?

a) .... **b)** ....

5 a) Circle the correct options in the following sentence:

During polymerisation, small **hydrogen / hydrocarbon / oxygen / nitrogen** molecules called

polymers / monomers / polythene / PVC join together to make very long molecules.

b) Complete the following diagram showing how a polymer forms.

6 How are crosslinks formed?

....

....

....

HT **7** What is a polymer called when the molecules are packed more closely together? Tick the correct option.

A Crosslink ⬭   **B** Crystalline polymer ⬭

C Plasticizer ⬭   **D** Covalent bond ⬭

8 What is a plasticizer?

....

....

....

9 **a)** What are the three phases of an LCA?

i) ....

ii) ....

iii) ....

b) Fill in the missing words to complete the sentence below:

Each part of the life cycle is assessed for its .... impact and the amount of

.... and .... used.

c) The main benefits of a new fibre include its strength, its attractiveness, its resistance to abrasion and its water resistance. Which one can't be tested scientifically?

....

10 What are the three main methods of waste disposal?

a) .... **b)** .... **c)** ....

Radiation and Life

The Electromagnetic Spectrum

The **electromagnetic spectrum** is a family of seven radiations, including **visible light**.

A **beam** of electromagnetic radiation contains **'packets'** of energy called **photons**.

Different radiations contain photons that carry **different amounts** of energy.

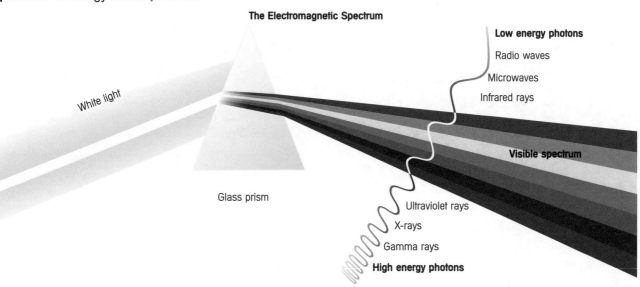

The Electromagnetic Spectrum

Transmitting Radiation

The general model of radiation shows how energy travels from a **source** which **emits** radiation, to a **detector** which **absorbs** radiation.

On the journey from **emitter** to **detector**, materials can **transmit, reflect** or **absorb** radiation.

For example, clouds absorb and reflect the Sun's energy, so on a cloudy day we receive less light than on a clearer day.

Emitter	Type of Waves	Detector
TV transmitter	Radio waves	TV aerial
Mobile phone mast	Microwaves	Mobile phones
The Sun	Light	The eye
Remote control	Infrared waves	Television
Some stars (e.g. supernova)	Gamma rays	Gamma ray telescope
X-ray machine	X-rays	Photographic plate

Intensity and Heat

The **intensity** of electromagnetic radiation is the energy arriving at a **surface per second**.

Intensity depends on the number of photons delivered per second and the amount of energy each packet contains, i.e. the photon energy.

The intensity of a beam **decreases** with distance, so the further from a source you are, the lower the intensity.

When a material absorbs radiation, heat is created. The amount of heat depends on its intensity.

Key Words

Electromagnetic spectrum • Ion • Photon

HT Intensity and Heat

The decrease in intensity is due to three factors:
- Photons **spread out** as they travel.
- Some photons are **absorbed** by particles in the substances they pass through.
- Some photons are **reflected** and **scattered** by other particles.

These factors **combine** to reduce the number of photons arriving per second at a detector. This results in a **lower measured intensity**.

When a material absorbs radiation, heat is created; the amount of heat depends on its intensity.

The amount of heat created depends on…
- the **intensity** of the radiation beam
- the **duration** of the exposure.

Ionising Radiation

Ionising radiation (electromagnetic radiation with a high photon energy) can break molecules into bits called **ions**. **Ultraviolet** radiation, **X-rays** and **gamma rays** are examples of ionising radiation.

HT Ions are **very reactive** and can easily take part in other chemical reactions.

Cell Damage

Radiation **damages** living cells in different ways:
- The heating effect can damage the skin, e.g. sunburn.
- Ionising radiation can age the skin. It can also **mutate** DNA, which can lead to cancer.
- Different amounts of exposure can cause different effects, e.g. high intensity ionising radiation can destroy cells, leading to **radiation poisoning**.

Microwaves can heat materials by causing the water particles to vibrate. There may be a health risk from the low intensity microwaves of mobile phones and masts, but this is disputed. One study found no link from short-term use but other studies have found some correlation.

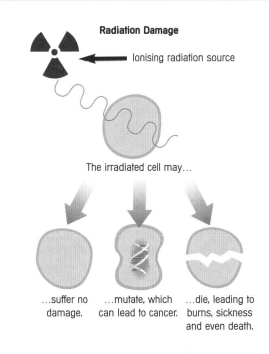

Radiation and Life

Radiation Protection

Microwave ovens have a metal case and a wire screen in the door to absorb microwaves and stop too much radiation escaping.

Other **physical barriers** are used to protect people:
- X-ray technicians use **lead screens**.
- Sunscreens and clothing can absorb ultraviolet radiation to help prevent skin cancer.
- Nuclear reactors are encased in thick lead and concrete.

People going into areas of high radiation must wear a **radiation suit** as a shield.

The Sun and the Ozone Layer

Light radiation from the Sun…
- warms the Earth's surface
- is used by plants for **photosynthesis**.

Photosynthesis **counteracts** respiration – it removes carbon dioxide and adds oxygen.

The **ozone layer** is a thin layer of gas in the Earth's upper atmosphere. It absorbs some of the Sun's ultraviolet radiation before it reaches Earth.

Without the ozone layer, the amount of radiation reaching Earth would be **very harmful**. Living organisms, especially animals, would suffer cell damage.

(HT) The energy from ultraviolet radiation causes chemical changes in the upper atmosphere when it's absorbed by the ozone layer. These changes are **reversible**.

The Greenhouse Effect

The Earth emits electromagnetic radiation into space. Gases in the atmosphere absorb some of the radiation and this keeps Earth warmer than it would be. This is known as the **greenhouse effect**.

Carbon dioxide (a **greenhouse gas**) makes up a small amount of Earth's atmosphere.

(HT) Other greenhouse gases include **water vapour** and trace amounts of **methane**.

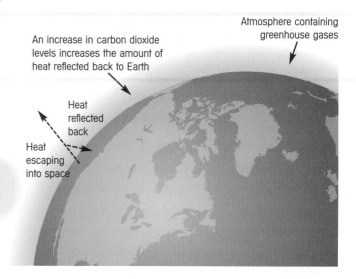

Atmosphere containing greenhouse gases

An increase in carbon dioxide levels increases the amount of heat reflected back to Earth

Heat reflected back

Heat escaping into space

The Carbon Cycle

The **carbon cycle** is an example of a balanced system.

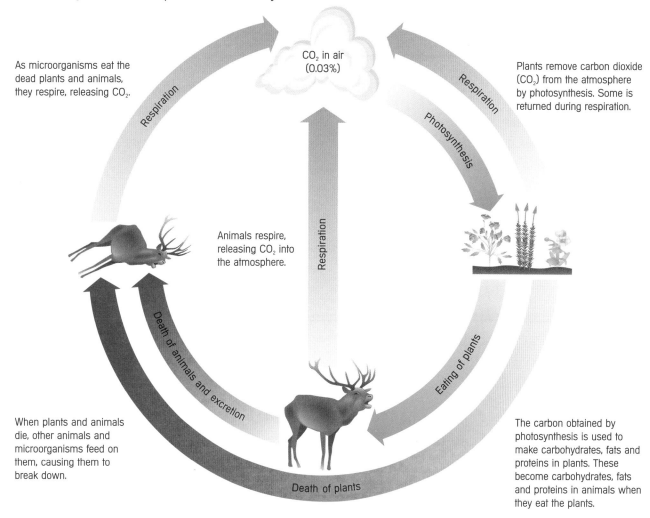

As microorganisms eat the dead plants and animals, they respire, releasing CO_2.

Respiration

CO_2 in air (0.03%)

Respiration

Photosynthesis

Plants remove carbon dioxide (CO_2) from the atmosphere by photosynthesis. Some is returned during respiration.

Animals respire, releasing CO_2 into the atmosphere.

Respiration

Death of animals and excretion

Eating of plants

When plants and animals die, other animals and microorganisms feed on them, causing them to break down.

Death of plants

The carbon obtained by photosynthesis is used to make carbohydrates, fats and proteins in plants. These become carbohydrates, fats and proteins in animals when they eat the plants.

Using the Carbon Cycle

The carbon cycle can be used to explain several points:

- Carbon dioxide (CO_2) levels in the Earth's atmosphere remained roughly **constant** for thousands of years because it was constantly being **recycled** by plants and animals.
- **Decomposers** are important microorganisms that break down dead material and release CO_2.
- CO_2 levels in the atmosphere have been steadily increasing, largely due to human activity, e.g. burning **fossil fuels** and **deforestation**.

- Burning fossil fuels releases carbon that was removed from the atmosphere millions of years ago and had been 'locked up' ever since.
- Burning forests not only release carbon, but also reduces the number of plants removing CO_2 from the atmosphere.

Key Words

Carbon cycle • Decomposer • Deforestation • Greenhouse effect • Ozone layer • Photosynthesis

Radiation and Life

Global Warming

The increase in greenhouse gases in the Earth's atmosphere means the amount of absorbed radiation from the Sun increases. This causes the Earth's temperature to increase, an effect known as **global warming**, which may lead to…

- **climate change** – crops may not be able to grow in some areas
- **extreme weather**, e.g. hurricanes
- **rising sea levels** – melting ice caps and higher sea temperatures may cause sea levels to rise, flooding low-lying land.

(HT) Data about the Earth's changing temperature is collected and used with climate models to look for **patterns** in the possible causes of global **warming**.

These computer models show that one of the main global warming factors is the rise in carbon dioxide levels in the atmosphere, providing evidence that human activity is to blame.

Risk and Benefit

All new advances have the potential for **risk**. Radiation advances are unlikely to be risk-free.

For example, until a correlation between mobile phones and cancer can be proved, people need to make their own decisions and evaluate the risks against the **benefits**.

Another example of risk, benefit and control is X-rays. Although X-rays allow doctors to make a much more **accurate** diagnosis, their exposure times have to be controlled.

X-ray radiation can destroy cancerous cells, but it can harm healthy cells too.

(HT) A study may show a **correlation** (link) between a **factor** and an **outcome**. But this does not mean that the factor will always cause the outcome.

For example, there may be a link between mobile phones (factor) and cancer (outcome). But using a mobile phone will not always lead to cancer.

Some people say it's better to take **precautionary measures**, e.g. limit usage, especially for young people.

Benefits of Mobile Phones

- Easy convenient method of communication, especially when vulnerable, e.g. if your car breaks down.
- Easy way to keep in contact.

Risks of Mobile Phones

- Some studies have linked mobile phones to brain tumours.
- Studies are still being carried out and the long-term effects aren't known.

Risk Reduction

- Limit usage to emergencies and texting.
- Use a hands-free kit.
- Avoid using when the signal's low.

Weighing the Risks

In weighing up a risk it's important to consider the chance of the **outcome** and any **consequences**. Although a risk may seem low, the outcome could be very serious.

For example, although there's evidence that prolonged exposure to ultraviolet light increases the risk of skin cancer, many people still sunbathe. Some reasons could be that…

- sunlight is needed for good health and is a source of vitamin D
- sunlight can help prevent SAD (seasonal affective disorder) and skin conditions such as eczema
- people think a tan looks healthy or attractive
- people think it will not happen to them.

HT The ALARA Principle

Actual risk is a **scientific measure** of the dangers of something. **Perceived risk** is how dangerous people think it is.

These **values** can be very different. Factors that affect perceived risk include…

- media coverage and personal bias
- social influence, e.g. opinions of family.

The ALARA (**As Low As Reasonably Achievable**) principle is used as a guideline for **risk management**. It states that measures should be taken to make the risks as small as possible, whilst still providing the **benefits** and taking into account **social, economic** and **practical implications**. For example, this is used in radiology units to protect staff, and to control the dose of radiation given in each treatment.

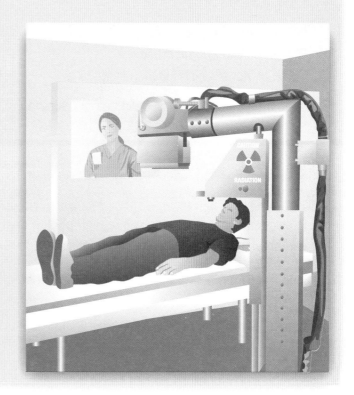

Key Words

ALARA • Global warming • Risk

Module P2 Summary

The Electromagnetic Spectrum

The **electromagnetic spectrum** = seven radiations, including **visible light**.

A **beam** of electromagnetic radiation contains **photons**.

Different radiations contain photons that carry **different amounts** of **energy**.

Transmitting Radiation

Emitter (a source of radiation) ➡ **Detector** (absorbs radiation)

Radiation energy travels from an emitter to a detector — materials can **transmit**, **reflect** or **absorb** this radiation.

Intensity and Heat

Intensity of **electromagnetic radiation** = energy arriving at a **surface per second**.

Intensity depends on the **number of photons** delivered **per second** and the **amount of photon energy**.

The intensity of a beam **decreases** with distance. The further from a source you are, the **lower** the intensity.

Heat is created when a material **absorbs** radiation — the **amount** of heat depends on the intensity.

HT Three factors can **combine** to cause a decrease in intensity:
- Photons **spread** as they travel.
- Some photons are **absorbed**.
- Some photons are **reflected**.

The amount of heat created depends on the **duration** of **exposure**.

Ionising Radiation

Ionising radiation…
- is electromagnetic radiation with a **high photon energy**
- can break molecules into **bits** called **ions**.

HT Ions are **very reactive** and can easily take part in other reactions.

Ionising Radiation and Health

Different amounts of exposure can cause different effects. **High intensity** ionising radiation can destroy cells leading to **radiation poisoning**.

There may be a **health risk** from microwaves in mobile phone use.

Physical barriers protect people in areas of high radiation, such as **radiation suits**.

The Sun and the Ozone Layer

Light radiation from the **Sun** warms Earth and is used in **photosynthesis**.

The **ozone layer** absorbs **ultraviolet radiation** before it reaches Earth ➡ Without this layer the radiation would be very **harmful**.

The Greenhouse Effect

Greenhouse effect = Gases in the atmosphere absorb radiation and keep the Earth warmer than it would be.

Carbon dioxide = a **greenhouse gas**.

HT Other greenhouse gases include **water vapour** and **methane**.

Global Warming

Global warming causes **climate change**, **extreme weather** and **rising sea levels**.

The **increase** in greenhouse gases in the atmosphere means the temperature of the Earth **increases**.

HT Computer climate models use data to look for patterns to find the cause of global warming.

The rise in carbon dioxide levels has been shown to be a factor in global warming ➡ Human activity is to blame.

The Carbon Cycle

The **carbon cycle** is a balanced system:
1. **Plants** remove **carbon dioxide** from the atmosphere.
2. Carbon from photosynthesis makes **carbohydrates**, **fats** and **proteins**.
3. Animals and microorganisms feed on dead animals to **break them down**.
4. Microorganisms and animals **respire**, releasing carbon dioxide.

Carbon dioxide levels once remained constant – they were **recycled** by plants and animals. Levels have risen because of **human activity**, e.g. deforestation.

Risk and Benefit

Radiation advances are unlikely to be **risk-free**. Until a correlation is **proven**, people need to assess the **risks** against the **benefits**.

HT **ALARA** = As Low As Reasonably Achievable

ALARA – a guideline for **risk management**.

Module P2 Practice Questions

1 Circle the correct options in the following sentences:

a) A **beam / photon / packet / ion** of electromagnetic radiation contains **beams / photons / packets / ions** of energy called **beams / photons / packets / ions**.

b) Radiation energy travels from a source known as the **detector / photon / emitter / spectrum** to a **detector / photon / emitter / spectrum**.

2 a) Fill in the missing words to complete the sentence below:

Intensity depends on the number of .... delivered per ....

and the amount of .... each .... contains.

b) Which of the following statements is true? Tick the correct option.

A The intensity of a beam of light decreases with distance. ⬜

B The intensity of a beam of light never changes with distance. ⬜

C The intensity of a beam of light energises with distance. ⬜

D The intensity of a beam of light increases with distance. ⬜

HT c) Give three factors that combine to reduce the intensity of radiation delivered by the Sun to the Earth's surface.

i) ....

ii) ....

iii) ....

3 Name two examples of ionising radiation.

a) ....

b) ....

4 Give two examples of how radiation can damage cells.

a) ....

b) ....

5 **a)** What is the thin layer of gas in the Earth's upper atmosphere called?

....

b) How does this protect the Earth?

....

c) What would be the consequences if this layer did not exist?

....

....

HT **d)** Fill in the missing word to complete the sentence below:

Ultraviolet radiation causes .... chemical changes in the upper atmosphere.

6 **a)** Why did carbon dioxide levels remain constant for thousands of years?

....

b) Give two reasons why carbon dioxide levels have now started increasing.

i) ....

ii) ....

7 Name three consequences of global warming, and give an example for each.

a) Consequence: ....   Example: ....

b) Consequence: ....   Example: ....

c) Consequence: ....   Example: ....

HT **8** **a)** What do the letters ALARA stand for?

....

b) Explain the ALARA principle.

....

....

Life on Earth

Life on Earth

Life on Earth began about **3500 million** years ago.

During that time there has been a large number of species living on Earth, many of which are now **extinct**.

A species is a group of organisms which can freely breed with each other to produce fertile offspring.

The very first living things developed from **simple molecules** that could **copy** or **replicate** themselves.

It's not known whether these molecules...

- were produced by conditions on Earth at the time (harsh surface conditions, or in deep sea vents), or
- arrived on Earth from an external source, e.g. a comet hitting Earth.

Experiments have simulated the harsh conditions on Earth millions of years ago, which led to **simple organic molecules** developing.

There's evidence of simple organic molecules existing in gas clouds in space and in comets.

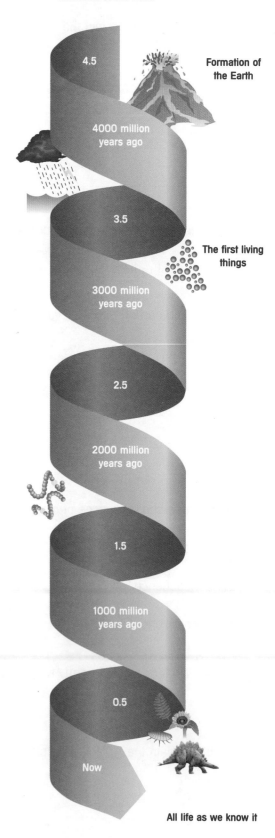

Timescale of the Earth

4.5

Formation of the Earth

4000 million years ago

3.5

The first living things

3000 million years ago

2.5

2000 million years ago

1.5

1000 million years ago

0.5

Now

All life as we know it

Key Words

Common ancestor • DNA • Evolution • Fossil • Natural selection

The Beginning of Life

Evidence suggests that all existing organisms share certain traits, including **cellular structure** and the **genetic** code, **DNA**. This would mean that all existing organisms share a **common ancestor** and evolved from very simple living things. Two sources of evidence support this: the **fossil** record and DNA evidence.

The Fossil Record

Fossil evidence supports the common ancestor theory and shows the history of species and the evolutionary changes over millions of years.

Fossils can be formed from the…

- hard parts of organisms that don't decay easily
- parts of animals and plants which haven't decayed because one or more of the conditions needed for decay were absent, e.g. oxygen or moisture
- soft parts of organisms which can be replaced by minerals as they decay. This can preserve traces of footprints or burrows.

Evolution of Ammonites

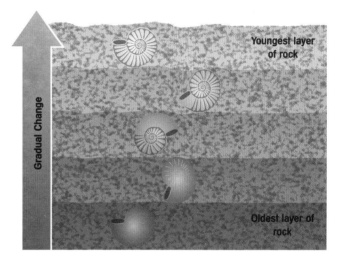

Gradual Change

Youngest layer of rock

Oldest layer of rock

DNA Evidence

DNA evidence also supports the common ancestor theory. Analysing DNA of both living organisms and fossils shows the similarities and the differences.

This can be used to fill gaps in the **fossil record**. The more shared genes organisms have, the more closely related they are. Comparing **gene sequences** reveals that the DNA of some organisms is very similar to organisms that seem very different.

For example, human DNA shares 98.8% of chimpanzee DNA, our nearest genetic relative. A mouse, which appears very dissimilar from humans, shares 85% of chimpanzee DNA.

This evidence suggests that **evolution** by **natural selection** made life as it is today. If conditions on Earth had been different, then the results could have been very different.

Mouse   **Chimpanzee**   **Human**

Life on Earth

Evolution by Natural Selection

Evolution…

- is the slow, continual change over generations
- may result in a new species which is **better adapted** to its environment
- occurs due to **natural selection**, when individuals have characteristics which improve their chances of survival.

Four key points about natural selection:

1. Individuals show **variation**, i.e. differences due to their genes.
2. There's **competition** for food and mates. Also, disease and predators keep population sizes constant in spite of many offspring.
3. Those better adapted are more likely to survive and reproduce whilst others die out. This is '**survival of the fittest**'.
4. Survivors pass on genes to their offspring, resulting in an improved organism evolving over generations.

Natural selection relies on variation caused by the environment and genes. However, only a **genetic variation** can be passed on. For example, if you lost a finger, this characteristic wouldn't be passed on. This is **environmental variation**.

Increased competition has seen grey squirrels outnumber red squirrels.

(HT) Peppered Moths are naturally pale and speckled, so are well camouflaged against silver birch trees.

However, during the Industrial Revolution, air pollution discoloured the trees with soot and natural selection led to a **new variety** of Peppered Moth:

1. **Variation** – some moths were naturally darker due to their genes.
2. **Competition** – darker-coloured and paler moths had to compete for food.
3. **Better adapted** – darker moths were better camouflaged against the blackened trees and buildings. Paler moths were seen by birds and were eaten.
4. **Passing on genes** – darker moths were more likely to survive and breed, passing on their genes for darker pigmentation.

The Clean Air Act reduced air pollution which meant more silver birch trees stayed 'silver'. This gave the pale variety an advantage so numbers began to grow again. Today, the presence of the pale variety is regarded as a clean air marker.

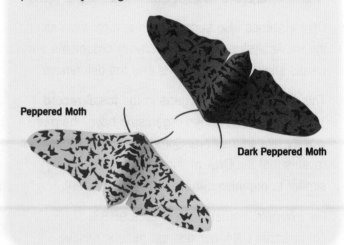

Peppered Moth

Dark Peppered Moth

Key Words

Competition • Environmental variation • Evolution • Mutation • Natural selection • Selective breeding • Survival of the fittest

HT Gene Mutation

A change in a gene is a **mutation**. Occasionally, mutations can alter the properties of a **protein** and can influence the **development** of an organism.

If this happens in a **sex cell** then the mutated gene can be passed on to the offspring, which may show **new characteristics**.

A new species can be produced through the combined effects of **mutations**, **environmental changes** and **natural selection**.

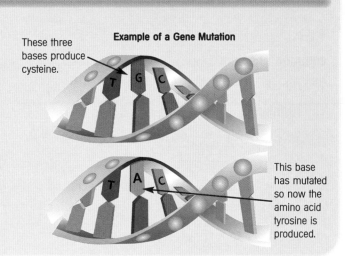

Example of a Gene Mutation

These three bases produce cysteine.

This base has mutated so now the amino acid tyrosine is produced.

Selective Breeding

Selective breeding is when animals with certain traits are mated to produce offspring with certain desirable characteristics. Selective breeding can produce two outcomes:

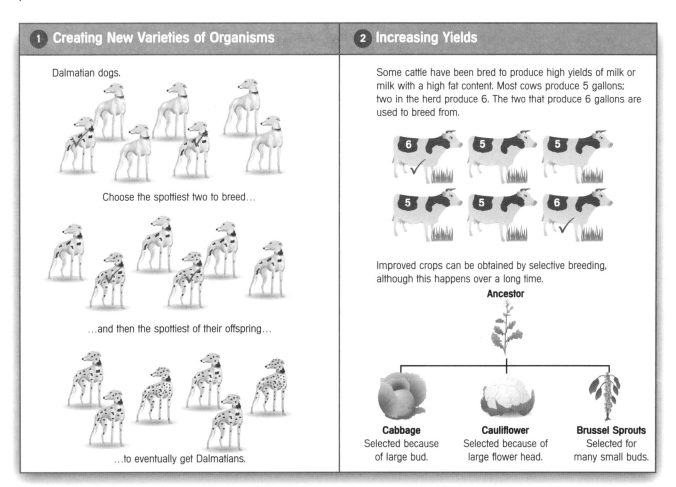

1 Creating New Varieties of Organisms

Dalmatian dogs.

Choose the spottiest two to breed…

…and then the spottiest of their offspring…

…to eventually get Dalmatians.

2 Increasing Yields

Some cattle have been bred to produce high yields of milk or milk with a high fat content. Most cows produce 5 gallons; two in the herd produce 6. The two that produce 6 gallons are used to breed from.

6 ✓ 5 5
5 5 6 ✓

Improved crops can be obtained by selective breeding, although this happens over a long time.

Ancestor

Cabbage
Selected because of large bud.

Cauliflower
Selected because of large flower head.

Brussel Sprouts
Selected for many small buds.

Life on Earth

The Evolution of Humans

It's thought that apes and humans share a **common ancestor**. The investigation of **fossil records** was the basis of this idea.

The **Hominid** family, i.e. humans, gorillas and orangutans, **branched** during evolution and several Homo species developed.

Homo sapiens is now the only living species of its type and other Homo species are now **extinct**.

Natural selection is most likely to have caused hominids' brain size to **increase** over time because…
- there's a rough correlation between brain size and intelligence
- large brains would give individuals an advantage, making them more likely to survive.

It was originally thought that brain size would have increased before hominids began walking upright. However, fossil evidence suggests that walking upright came first.

This shows the role of observations and data in establishing the **reliability** of an explanation.

If new observations or data agree with a theory it increases confidence in the explanation.

HT However, it doesn't necessarily prove that the theory is correct.

If new observations or data disagree, it indicates that either the observations or data are wrong, or the theory is wrong.

HT This may, therefore, decrease our confidence in the explanation.

When this happens, further investigations are carried out to establish where the error lies. If the new observations or data prove reliable, then the theory will be revised. This is how scientific explanations change over time.

Members of the Homo Group

Common Ancestor
Homo habilis
(evidence exists they were the earliest ancestor, using simple tools)

Common Ancestor
Homo erectus
(had large brains and may have used fire to cook)

Cousin
Homo neanderthalensis
(close cousin of *Homo sapiens*)

Cousin
Homo sapiens
(present-day humans)

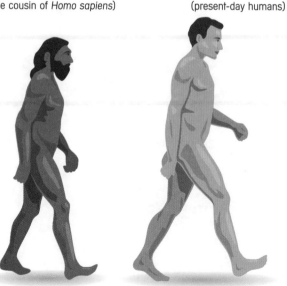

Origins of Life

How life on Earth began has long been debated:

- Religions say God, or a creator, created all life.
- Scientists have testable theories that try to explain similarities between organisms.

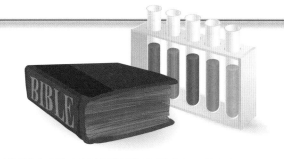

Inheritance of Acquired Characteristics

Jean-Baptiste Lamarck devised the theory that an animal evolved over its lifetime; the more an animal used part of its body, the more it would adapt. For example, a giraffe stretching for leaves would develop a long neck.

A scientist called Weismann cast doubt on Lamarck's theory. He cut the tails off mice and bred them. The mice produced offspring with tails, conflicting with Lamarck's explanation.

However, Lamarck said Weismann's experiment was deliberate mutation and that only situations where the animal desired change were valid.

Lamarck used **imagination** and **creativity** to develop his explanation, but Weismann's evidence led to the **rejection** of Lamarck's theory.

HT Scientific explanations are not abandoned when conflicting data is found because…

- new data may be incorrect
- explanations based on new data can run into problems
- many scientists will have based work on the existing explanation and will stick with it.

A new explanation is only likely to replace another once it's proven to be reliable.

Evolution by Natural Selection

In the 1830s Charles Darwin created a testable **theory of evolution**, studying different types of finch on the Galapagos Islands.

Darwin made four important observations for his theory: **variety**, **competition**, **survival of the fittest**, and **passing on desirable characteristics**.

HT Darwin linked these observations and deduced that the **best-adapted** organisms would **survive** and **reproduce**. This was the basis of his theory of **'Evolution by Natural Selection'**.

Scientists can't ever be certain how life began; evidence is scarce and theories are based on the evidence available at the time. New discoveries are still being made and developing our scientific knowledge.

Key Words

Common ancestor • Hominid • Theory of Evolution

Life on Earth

The Extinction of Species

Species have become **extinct** over time, e.g. the dodo. The usual cause is a species' inability to adapt to change in the form of…

- **increased competition**
- new **predators**
- change in the **environment**
- new **diseases**.

Mass extinctions…

- are when many species disappear in a relatively short time
- occur when environmental change happens so quickly that animals and plants can't adapt fast enough.

Human activity has been responsible for the extinction of some species. For example…

- the introduction of new predators or competition, e.g. mitten crabs travelled in ships to the UK, where they eat native species of crab
- industrial activities causing global warming
- deforestation clears areas, increases carbon dioxide levels and alters the carbon cycle.

The Dodo

Extinctions Caused Directly by Man

The **Great Auk** (a sea bird)…

- only laid one egg a year and couldn't fly, so was vulnerable
- was hunted for food and its down. The last pair was killed in 1844.

The **smallpox** virus…

- was eradicated deliberately by man by mass vaccination
- was declared extinct in 1980. The only examples are stored in two laboratories.

Extinctions Caused Indirectly by Man

The **Rodrigues pigeon**…

- was native to Rodrigues Island in the Indian Ocean
- became extinct when ships visiting the island accidently introduced rats, which preyed on the birds.

The **Gould's Mouse**…

- disappeared rapidly after Europeans settled in Australia – they were affected by changes to their habitat
- was thought to have been hunted by cats and killed by diseases from rats and mice (which were introduced by man).

Maintaining Biodiversity

Every time a species becomes extinct, information stored in its genetic code is **lost**.

Projects like the Kew Gardens Millennium Seed Bank Project prevent this by collecting and storing seeds from all over the world.

Extinctions mean **less variety** on Earth. Without variety people would start to run out of food crops and medicines. Many medicines are developed from plants or animals. There are potentially many medicines in areas like the Amazon rainforest – an area rapidly undergoing deforestation.

By understanding how our actions can impact on **biodiversity**, scientists hope to discover ways to use the Earth's resources in a **sustainable** way.

Food Chains

Organisms don't live in isolation. Different species of animals or plants compete for resources in the same habitat.

Food chains can show the feeding relationships between organisms. When animals eat plants or other animals, energy is passed up the food chain.

Animals are dependent upon each other and their environment for survival.

For example, if rabbits became extinct, then the stoat and the fox may be at risk. Their numbers may then be reduced as competition for food increased.

Food Webs

Food webs…
- show how all the food chains in a habitat are **inter-related**
- can be complicated as many animals have **varied** diets.

Environmental changes can alter the food web. For example, less rain could reduce the amount of lettuces and cause reductions in slug numbers.

If the changes are too great, organisms will die before they can reproduce, eventually becoming extinct.

Food Web

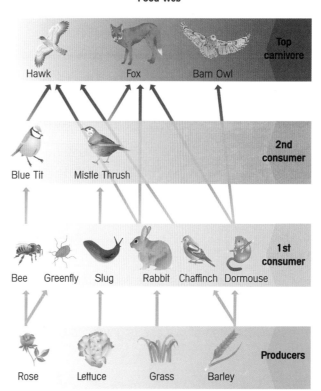

Hawk   Fox   Barn Owl   **Top carnivore**

Blue Tit   Mistle Thrush   **2nd consumer**

Bee   Greenfly   Slug   Rabbit   Chaffinch   Dormouse   **1st consumer**

Rose   Lettuce   Grass   Barley   **Producers**

Key Words

Extinct • Biodiversity • Sustainable • Food chain • Food web

Life on Earth

Communication Systems

The evolution of **multi-cellular** organisms eventually led to the development of nervous and hormonal **communication systems**.

Nerve impulses are **electrical signals**. They are **rapid** and **short-lived**.

Hormone signals are **chemical** messages in the blood. They are **slow-acting** and **longer-lasting** than nerve impulses.

Hormones regulate the functions of many organs and cells.

HT The maintenance of a constant internal body environment (temperature, etc.) is called **homeostasis.**

The body uses nervous signals and hormonal signals to ensure the systems are stable.

Hormones and Human Fertility

Human fertility is an example of hormone communication. A woman produces hormones that cause an egg to mature and be released:

1. Follicle stimulating hormone (FSH) from the **pituitary gland** causes the ovaries to produce oestrogen and an egg to mature. There are changes in the thickness of the lining of the womb.
2. Oestrogen, produced in the ovaries, inhibits the production of FSH and causes the production of luteinising hormone (LH).
3. LH, also from the pituitary gland, stimulates the release of an egg in the middle of the menstrual cycle.

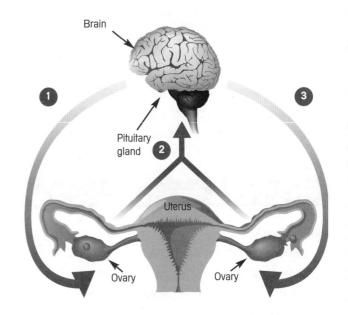

Hormones and Insulin

The body's use of **insulin** is an example of hormone communication. The pancreas produces insulin. Its level in the blood is governed by the amount of **glucose** in the blood:

- If the glucose concentration increases, insulin is released into the bloodstream.
- The insulin causes cells to take in the glucose.
- Any additional glucose is stored as glycogen.

The transportation of glucose is governed by the circulatory system.

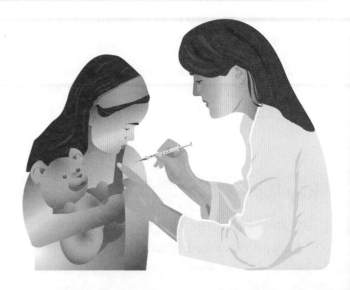

The Central Nervous System

The nervous system is based around…
- **sensor** (receptor) cells that detect stimuli
- **effector** cells that respond to the stimuli.

Neurones (nerve cells) connect the sensor cells (e.g. in the eyes, ears and skin) and effector cells (e.g. muscles, glands) together. Neurones are specially adapted cells that carry an electrical signal impulse.

The coordination of the nervous system in humans, and other vertebrates, is carried out by the **central nervous system**, which consists of the spinal cord and brain.

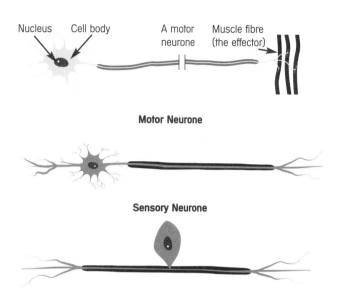

Nucleus   Cell body   A motor   Muscle fibre
                             neurone   (the effector)

Motor Neurone

Sensory Neurone

Involuntary Responses to Stimuli

Removing your hand from a pin is an example of an **involuntary or reflex nervous action**.

1 A receptor is stimulated by the drawing pin, which is the **stimulus**.

2 This causes **impulses** to pass along a **sensory neurone** into the **spinal cord**.

3 The sensory neurone **synapses** (communicates) with a **relay neurone**, bypassing the brain.

4 The relay neurone synapses with a **motor neurone**, sending impulses down it.

5 These impulses reach the **effectors** (muscles), causing them to contract and remove the hand in response to the sharp drawing pin.

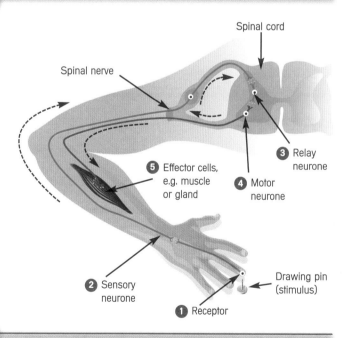

Spinal cord

Spinal nerve

3 Relay neurone

5 Effector cells, e.g. muscle or gland

4 Motor neurone

2 Sensory neurone

Drawing pin (stimulus)

1 Receptor

Voluntary Responses to Stimuli

Turning down loud music is an example of a **voluntary nervous reaction**.

Sound-sensitive receptors detect loud music. Sensory neurones pass an electrical signal to the central nervous system where the information is processed.

A response, in the form of another electrical signal, is sent by the motor neurone to the effector cells in the muscles in the arms and fingers.

The arm and finger muscles respond by covering the ears to block the sound and then turning the volume down.

Key Words

Central nervous system • Effector • Hormone • Neurone • Sensor • Stimulus

Module B3 Summary

Life on Earth

Life on Earth began about **3500 million years ago**.

The very first living things developed from **simple molecules** that could **replicate** themselves.

It's not known whether the molecules were produced on Earth or from an **external source**.

Common Ancestors

Evidence suggests all existing organisms…
* have a **common ancestor**
* share **cellular structure** and **genetic code**.

DNA and Fossil Evidence

The common ancestor theory is supported by…
* **fossil evidence** – shows the **evolutionary changes** over millions of years
* **DNA evidence** – shows the **similarities** between organisms.

The more shared genes organisms have, the more **closely related** they are.

Evolution by Natural Selection

Evolution = a slow, continual change over generations.

Evolution by **natural selection** made life as it is today. If conditions had been different then the results could have been **very different**.

In natural selection…
* individuals show **variation**
* there's **competition** for food and mates
* those **better adapted** will survive – '**Survival of the fittest**'
* survivors **pass on** their genes

Natural selection relies on variation caused by the **environment** and **genes**.

Only **genetic variations** can be passed on. **Environmental variations** aren't passed on.

HT Gene Mutation

A change in a gene is a **mutation**.

Mutations can **alter the properties** of a protein and **influence the development** of an organism.

A **new species** can be produced through the combined effects of **mutations**, **environmental changes** and **natural selection**.

Module B3 Summary

The Evolution of Humans

The **Hominid** family **branched** during evolution ➡ Several Homo species developed.

Homo sapiens is now the only living species of its type.

Hominds' brain size would have **increased** over time, making them more likely to survive. There's a rough **correlation** between brain size and intelligence.

Fossil evidence suggests that walking upright came before brain size increased.

The Extinction of Species

Species have become **extinct** over time.

Extinctions are usually caused by an inability to adapt to…
*   increased **competition**
*   new **predators**
*   **environmental changes**
*   **new diseases**.

Mass extinctions are when many species disappear quickly because organisms can't adapt fast enough.

Human activity has been responsible for the extinction of some species and can affect **biodiversity − less variety** on Earth.

Food chains and **food webs** can show how organisms' diets in a habitat are **inter-related**.

Nerves and Hormones

Nerve impulses are **electrical**, **rapid** and **short-lived**.

Hormone signals are **chemical**, **slow** and **longer-lasting**.

(HT) The maintenance of a constant internal body environment is called **homeostasis**.

The **nervous system** is based around **sensors** and **receptors**. These are connected by specially-adapted cells called **neurones** that carry **electrical signals**.

The **central nervous system** consists of the **spinal cord** and **brain**.

Scientific Explanation

Observations and data are important to reach a reliable explanation.

Investigations are carried out to test a theory. If the results disagree, further investigations try to establish where the error lies.

Module B3 Practice Questions

1 How long ago is it thought that life first began on Earth?

_____

2 Give two pieces of evidence to support the suggestion that all existing organisms have a common ancestor.

a) _____

b) _____

3 **a)** Fill in the missing words to complete the sentences below:

Fossils show the _____ of species and the _____ changes

over millions of years.

b) Analysing _____ can be used to fill gaps in the fossil record.

c) The more shared _____ organisms have, the more closely

_____ they are.

4 Evolution occurs through natural selection. Which of the following factors are necessary for natural selection to occur? Tick the four correct options.

A Variation ◯   **B** Attractive colours ◯

C Better adapted ◯   **D** Pass on genes ◯

E Competition ◯   **F** Similarities ◯

G Good communication ◯   **H** High DNA content ◯

5 What is environmental variation? Give an example of this.

_____

_____

_____

6 Circle the correct options in the following sentence:

Selective breeding is when animals and plants with certain traits are deliberately **separated / mutated / mated / evolved** to provide offspring with desirable **organisms / characteristics / cells / structures**.

7 Give three reasons why a species may become extinct.

a) ....

b) ....

c) ....

8 Maintaining biodiversity is important. Circle the correct options in the following sentence:

Biodiversity is important because without **competition / characteristics / variety / evolution** we would run out of food, medicines and **variety / characteristics / resources / competition**.

9 Construct a food chain using **Greenfly**, **Blackbird**, **Oak tree** and **Ladybird**. Write the name of each organism in the correct box below.

....	....	....	....

10 What are the two systems of sending messages in the body?

a) ....

b) ....

11 The diagram below shows the body's involuntary response to stimuli. Match statements **A–E** with the labels **1–5** on the diagram. Enter the appropriate number in the boxes provided.

A   Impulses pass along a sensory neurone into the spinal cord. ◯

B   The muscles contract in response to pain. ◯

C   A receptor is stimulated. ◯

D   The sensory neurone synapses with a relay neurone, bypassing the brain. ◯

E   The relay neurone synapses with a motor neurone, sending impulses down it. ◯

Food Matters

The Nitrogen Cycle

Nitrogen is a vital element in all living things. It's used in the production of **amino acids** and **proteins**, which…

- consist mainly of carbon, hydrogen, oxygen and nitrogen
- are needed for plants and animals to grow.

Fertile soil is needed for crops to grow. There's a **continual cycle** of elements through consumption of living organisms and decay.

The **nitrogen cycle** shows how nitrogen and its compounds are recycled in nature.

HT **Stages of the nitrogen cycle:**

1. Nitrogen-fixing bacteria convert atmospheric **nitrogen** into **nitrates** in soil. Some of these bacteria live in the soil, whilst others are found in the roots of leguminous plants (e.g. pea plants).
2. When plants are eaten the nitrogen becomes animal **protein.**
3. Dead organisms and waste contain **ammonium compounds.**
4. **Decomposers** convert **urea**, faeces and protein from dead organisms into **ammonium compounds.**
5. Nitrifying bacteria convert ammonium compounds into **nitrates** in the soil.
6. **Denitrifying bacteria** convert **nitrates** into **atmospheric nitrogen** and ammonium compounds.

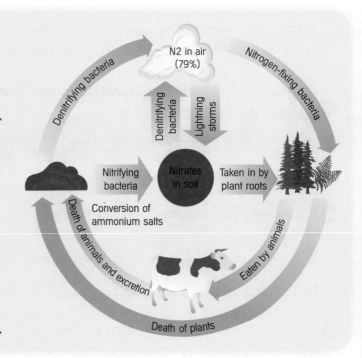

Intensive and Organic Farming

Farmers use **intensive farming** to produce more food at lower cost. Intensive farming…

- uses **fertilisers** and **pesticides**
- keeps animals in controlled environments with limited movement and regulated temperatures. Some people find this morally unacceptable.

Organic farming…

- uses more **natural methods** which have less environmental impact
- has **higher costs** and more farm workers need to be employed.

Farms must follow the UK national standards to be recognised as organic farms; the Soil Association is one of the agencies which monitors this.

Maintaining Fertile Soil

Land becomes less fertile when crops are harvested because plants **remove** nutrients, e.g. nitrogen from the soil. The nutrients are not returned through the natural process of decay. They can be replaced in different ways:

- Intensive farmers use manufactured fertilisers to replace the lost nutrients.
- Organic farmers use manure to add nutrients. They also rotate their crops.

HT Harvested crops also remove **potassium** and **phosphorus** from the soil.

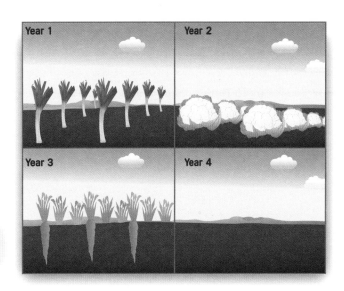

Crop Yields

Pests may carry disease and damage crops. This means fewer crops or a lower yield. Intensive farms use **pesticides** while organic farms use biological control (e.g. introducing a predator to kill a pest).

Intensive farms generally produce **high yields** at **low cost**, which benefits consumers. Organic farms are more **labour intensive** and produce **lower yields** at **higher costs**.

The Environment and Farming

Intensive farms...

- are often small, leaving room for woodland. However, hedgerows can be removed to maximise the amount of crops planted
- burn **fossil fuels** and use **fertilisers** and **pesticides** that can harm organisms that are not pests – pesticides can enter the food chain, passing toxins on.

Organic farms...

- have smaller fields with less destruction of hedgerows and don't affect food chains
- don't use pesticides and fertilisers so there's **less harm**, and there's more local employment. This is **sustainable development**.

HT There's a difference between what can be done and what should be done. Different social and economic circumstances need to be considered.

Key Words

Amino acid • Fertiliser • Intensive farming • Nitrogen cycle • Pesticide • Organic farming • Protein

Food Matters

Chemicals in Living Things

Your body is made up of cells, which are mainly **protein**. When you are growing, your body needs protein to make new cells. Protein is also needed by your body to **repair** old or damaged cells.

Proteins are compounds of carbon, hydrogen, oxygen and nitrogen. They are large molecules (polymers) made of lots of **amino acid** molecules joined together.

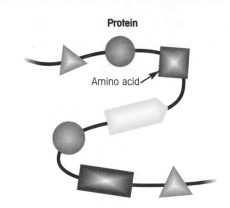

Protein

Amino acid

Chemicals in Food

Chemicals, or **additives**, are added to food for several reasons:

Additive	Reason
Colouring	Replaces colour which can be lost during processing or storage. Colourful food looks more attractive.
Flavouring	Gives a particular taste or replaces flavours lost during processing.
Emulsifier	Used to mix together ingredients that would normally separate, e.g. oil and water.
Stabiliser	Helps to stop ingredients from separating again.
Preservative	Stops mould or other microorganisms growing, so foods are kept safe and fresher for longer.
Sweetener	Used to reduce the amount of sugar added to processed foods and drinks.
Antioxidant	Stops foods containing fats or oils from reacting with oxygen in the air.

Health Concerns

An additive with an **E number** has passed a safety test and can be used in the UK and EU.

There are health concerns about food additives, e.g. some scientists think monosodium glutamate can have harmful effects.

Increased consumption of E numbers, especially amongst children, is thought to affect sleep patterns, behaviour, ability to concentrate and even IQ levels.

Toxins in Food

Many plants are eaten for food. Some contain natural chemicals that may be toxic and cause harm if not cooked properly. Others may give rise to allergies.

It's impossible to be completely safe because harmful chemicals can get into food many ways:

- Contamination during storage – moulds growing on cereals can produce a carcinogen called **aflatoxin**.
- Pesticides may be in the food we eat.
- Food processing and cooking may produce harmful chemicals.
- Poor storage of cooked food may result in contamination by bacteria, which can lead to food poisoning.

Plant	Natural Chemical	Effect
Cassava (a woody shrub)	Poisonous compounds release cyanide	Cyanide poisoning if eaten raw (Heating removes the toxin).
Wheat	Gluten	Damages the small intestine in people who suffer from intolerance (known as coeliac disease).
Peanuts	Proteins in the nuts	Allergic reaction from fresh, cooked and roasted peanuts as the proteins are not destroyed by cooking.

Reducing the Risk

You can reduce the **risk** of exposure to harmful chemicals in food by…

- keeping a hygienic kitchen and quickly disposing of waste food
- cooking food properly
- not refreezing previously frozen meats
- regularly cleaning the fridge to avoid keeping cooked foods too long
- reading food labels (particularly important for people with coeliac disease or allergies)
- buying organic food to avoid pesticides.

The risk from **different chemicals** in food can vary between people. For example, eating out is low-risk as there are **food hygiene laws** and kitchens must meet **Health and Safety standards**. But, it's not always possible to know the ingredients that have gone into preparing food. So, if you're allergic to a common ingredient such as nuts, eating out may be a **higher risk** for you than for others.

Key Words

Additive • E number • Risk

Food Matters

Food Standards Agency

The **Food Standards Agency** (FSA) is an independent food safety watchdog set up by an Act of Parliament in 2000. It...

- helps to make sure that food is safe, healthy and fairly marketed
- ensures that food producers act within the law
- promotes healthy eating and aims to minimise illnesses like food poisoning
- makes sure food labels are clear and say exactly what's in the food, e.g. coeliacs look for labels saying 'gluten free'.

The FSA uses **scientific advisory committees** to research issues, e.g. genetically modified (GM) foods. Sometimes the findings are controversial and the results debatable. This may result in further problems, e.g. manufacturers may not want to accept the findings as it may not be in their economic interest.

If there's any doubt about food safety then one of the committees is asked to carry out a **risk assessment** and decide...

- if the food contains harmful chemicals
- how harmful the chemicals are
- how much of the food must be eaten before it is likely to harm people
- if groups of people are vulnerable, e.g. children.

HT The Precautionary Principle

The outcome of a risk assessment is often based on experience gained from people eating the food.

Scientific evidence can be uncertain and the risks unknown, in which case the **precautionary principle** is applied:

- Experts and the public are consulted before the regulators make a decision.
- They weigh up the costs and benefits of any decision, as the priority is to protect the public and not just let new foods be put on sale.

For example, people ask if GM foods are safe to eat. Scientists don't yet know enough about the science of altering food genetically, which may lead to future health problems.

There's also not much data yet on the potential risks to humans, and this is why the precautionary principle is sometimes applied.

Digestion

Physical digestion includes chewing and squeezing food in the stomach:

- Food breaks into smaller pieces so it can pass through the gut.
- This increases the surface area of the food to help **enzymes** work faster.

Chemical digestion uses enzymes to break down large insoluble molecules into smaller soluble molecules:

- Smaller molecules can diffuse through the walls of the small intestines.
- They pass into the blood where they're transported around the body.

Enzymes in the saliva and stomach break down starch into glucose. The glucose is used in respiration to release energy.

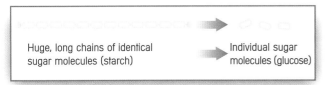

Huge, long chains of identical sugar molecules (starch) → Individual sugar molecules (glucose)

Other enzymes break down proteins into amino acids. The amino acids build or repair cells.

Cells take amino acids from the blood as they grow. The amino acids build up in the cells until proteins are made.

Many parts of the body consist mainly of proteins, including…

- **muscles**, **tendons**, **skin** and **hair**
- **haemoglobin** in the blood.

In a healthy person the excess amino acids are broken down in the liver and form **urea**. Blood transports urea to the kidneys where it's filtered out before being excreted in urine.

Proteins – huge, long chains of different amino acids → Amino acids

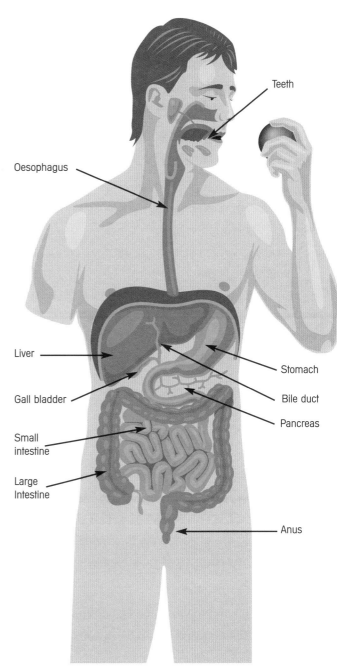

The Digestive System

Teeth

Oesophagus

Liver

Stomach

Gall bladder

Bile duct

Pancreas

Small intestine

Large Intestine

Anus

Key Words

Chemical digestion • Enzyme • Food Standards Agency • Physical digestion • Precautionary principle • Scientific advisory committee

Food Matters

Importance of a Healthy Diet

A **balanced diet** is important to stay healthy.

Eating the wrong foods can lead to disease. For example, **obesity** is a major problem, even amongst children. The main causes are…

- eating too much (especially fatty, sugary foods)
- not doing enough exercise.

Many people still over-eat and don't exercise, despite the link between heart disease and obesity.

People often think that they will not get heart disease and that the short-term benefits outweigh the risks. For example…

- foods high in fat, salt and sugar (e.g. crisps and sweets) taste good
- fruit and vegetables can be expensive
- exercising is hard work so people can't be bothered
- microwave meals are quick and easy whereas making fresh meals takes time.

HT How Healthy Are You?

Obese people are endangering their health and increasing their chances of heart disease, cancer and diabetes.

If you eat a lot of the wrong foods, you may be putting yourself at risk of obesity. You could ask yourself questions like…

- how healthy is my lifestyle?
- is there a family history of cancer, heart disease or diabetes, etc.?
- am I in a high risk age group?

If you're at high-risk and choose not to change your lifestyle, then you may later pay the consequences of poor health.

Diabetes

Processed foods can contain high levels of sugar. This is quickly absorbed into the bloodstream, causing a rapid rise in the **blood sugar** level.

Many people still eat too much processed food even though evidence suggests a link between one type of **diabetes** and **poor diet**.

Diabetes is caused by the **pancreas** not producing and releasing enough **insulin**. This allows the blood sugar level to fluctuate and can lead to a coma, or even death.

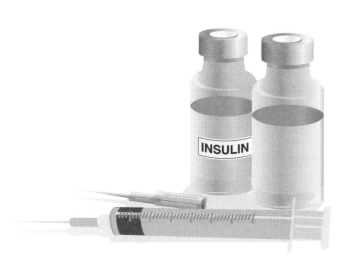

Types of Diabetes

There are two types of diabetes:

- **Type 1** is where the pancreas stops producing insulin altogether as the special cells in the pancreas are destroyed. This is more likely to start in young people and the blood sugar level can be controlled by injecting insulin.
- **Type 2** is where the pancreas doesn't make enough insulin or the cells don't respond to it. This can often be treated by diet and exercise.

The latter type is **late-onset diabetes** and more likely to start in older people. However, it's now being seen in younger people. This is because there are more obese young people. This group of people has a higher risk factor than those who are the correct weight and take regular exercise.

Other risk factors include **genetics** and **age**. For example, people in some ethnic groups are more likely to develop Type 2 diabetes at a younger age.

In a person with a fully functioning pancreas, if the blood glucose concentration is too high, the pancreas releases insulin.

Glucose from the blood is converted to insoluble glycogen in the liver.

Glycogen is removed from the blood.

The blood glucose concentration returns to normal.

Key Words

Blood sugar • Diabetes • Insulin • Pancreas

Module C3 Summary

The Nitrogen Cycle

Nitrogen is used in the production of **amino acids** and **proteins**.

Fertile soil is needed for **crops** to grow.

There's a **continual cycle** of elements through…
- **consumption** by **living organisms**
- **decay** of waste and dead organisms.

Nitrogen cycle = how nature recycles nitrogen and its compounds.

HT Stages of the Nitrogen Cycle
1. **Nitrogen-fixing bacteria** in soil convert nitrogen to nitrates.
2. When plants are eaten, **nitrogen** becomes **protein**.
3. Dead organisms contain **ammonium** compounds.
4. **Decomposers** convert dead organisms into ammonium compounds.
5. **Nitrifying bacteria** convert ammonium compounds into **nitrates**.
6. **Denitrifying bacteria** convert nitrates into ammonium compounds and nitrogen.

Maintaining Fertile Soil

Land becomes **less fertile** when crops are harvested because plants **remove nutrients** ➡ Nutrients aren't replaced naturally so farmers add **fertilisers**.

HT Harvested crops remove **potassium** and **phosphorus** from soil.

Intensive and Organic Farming

Intensive farms…
- produces **more food** at **lower cost**
- uses **fertilisers** and **pesticides**
- burn fossil fuels.

Organic farms…
- uses **natural methods** so there's less harm to the environment
- has **higher costs**
- produces **lower yields**
- must follow the UK national standards to be recognised as organic.

Chemicals in Living Things

Body cells are mainly **protein**.

Proteins are…
- needed to grow and to repair cells
- compounds of carbon, hydrogen, oxygen and nitrogen.

Chemicals in Food

Food **additives** are added to food...
- to improve colour, flavour, texture.
- to stabilise, preserve.

E numbers = food additives which have passed a safety test, though there are some health concerns.

Food and Risk

Some plants contain **toxic chemicals** that must be cooked properly to prevent harm.

Harmful chemicals can get into food in many ways:
- contamination in **storage**
- pesticides
- food processing.

Poor storage of cereals can produce **aflatoxin**, a carcinogen.

Risk of **exposure** to harmful chemicals can be reduced by:
- thoroughly cooking food
- keeping the kitchen and fridge clean
- buying organic
- reading food labels.

The risk from different chemicals can vary between people.

Food Standards Agency

Food Standards Agency (FSA) = food safety watchdog. It...
- helps make sure food is safe and healthy
- promotes healthy eating
- makes sure labels are clear.

Scientific advisory committees research issues about food safety ➡ Carry out **risk assessment**.

HT The Precautionary Principle

The **outcome** of a **risk assessment** is often based on people eating the food. If the risks are **unknown**, the **precautionary principle** is applied.

Experts and the public are consulted before a decision is made ➡ The **costs** and **benefits** to the public are then weighed up.

A Healthy Diet and Diabetes

A **balanced diet** is important to help stay healthy and prevent disease. Evidence suggests a link between **poor diet** and **diabetes**.

There are two types of **diabetes**:
- **Type 1** – pancreas stops producing **insulin** (need insulin injections).
- **Type 2** – pancreas doesn't make enough **insulin** or cells don't respond (treated by diet / exercise).

Module C3 Practice Questions

1 Fill in the missing words to complete the sentence below:

When plants take in nitrogen they use it to make .... acids

and ....

2 Which factors may reduce crop yield? Tick the four correct options.

A Lack of nutrients. ◯   **B** Pesticides. ◯

C Disease. ◯   **D** Fertilisers. ◯

E Too many nutrients. ◯   **F** Pests. ◯

3 a) What is the main difference between intensive farming and organic farming?

....

....

....

b) Name one advantage of…

i) Intensive farming ....

ii) Organic farming ....

4 Give three reasons why additives are put into food.

a) ....

b) ....

c) ....

5 Give two examples of steps you can take in the kitchen to reduce the risk of harmful chemicals in food.

a) ....

b) ....

6 Circle the correct options in the following sentence:

The FSA will ask a **production / scientific / departmental / local** advisory committee to decide if an

additive should be used and carry out a **manufacturer's / risk / production / advisory** assessment.

7 Is the following statement true or false?

Aflatoxin is the harmful substance that is formed by moulds on cereals when they are stored for a long time.

_____

8 Fill in the missing words to complete the sentences below:

a) _____ is broken down into _____ during digestion so that it's

small enough to pass through the _____ wall and be absorbed into the

_____ .

b) Hair, muscle and haemoglobin consist mainly of _____ .

9 a) What happens to the amino acids that our bodies don't need?

_____

b) Where does this process happen? Circle the correct option:

Pancreas   **Liver**   **Kidneys**   **Stomach**

10 Why is it important to have a balanced diet?

_____

_____

11 Why are sugary foods a problem for someone who is diabetic?

_____

_____

12 Circle the correct option in the following sentence:

Insulin is produced in the **pancreas / liver / kidneys / stomach**.

13 What factors can increase the risk of Type 2 diabetes? Tick the five correct options.

A Poor diet ◯   **B** Obesity ◯

C Age ◯   **D** Ethnicity ◯

E Regular exercise ◯   **F** Genetics ◯

G Where you live ◯   **H** Air quality ◯

Radioactive Materials

Atoms and Elements

All **elements** are made of **atoms**; each element contains only one type of atom. All atoms contain a **nucleus** and **electrons**.

The nucleus is made from **protons** and **neutrons**. Hydrogen (the lightest element) is the one exception. It has no neutrons; just one proton and one electron.

Helium Atom

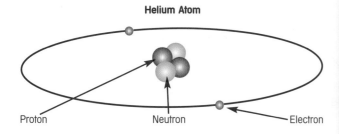

Proton   Neutron   Electron

Radioactive elements emit ionising radiation all the time. Neither chemical reactions nor physical processes (e.g. smelting) can change the radioactive behaviour of a substance.

HT Every atom of a **particular element** always has the same number of protons. (If it contained a different number of protons it would be a different element.) For example…
- hydrogen atoms have 1 proton
- helium atoms have 2 protons
- oxygen atoms have 8 protons.

However, some atoms of the same element can have **different numbers of neutrons** – these are **isotopes**. For example, there are three isotopes of oxygen:

Oxygen-16   Oxygen-17   Oxygen-18
has 8 neutrons   has 9 neutrons   has 10 neutrons.

NB: All three of these isotopes have 8 protons.

Ionising Radiation

Radioactive materials can give out three types of ionising radiation:
- **Alpha**
- **Beta**
- **Gamma**.

Different radioactive materials will give out any one, or a combination, of these radiations.

The different types of radiation have different penetrating powers.

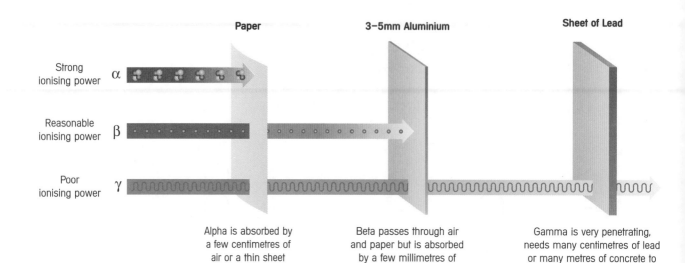

| Paper | 3–5mm Aluminium | Sheet of Lead |

Strong ionising power α

Reasonable ionising power β

Poor ionising power γ

Alpha is absorbed by a few centimetres of air or a thin sheet of paper.

Beta passes through air and paper but is absorbed by a few millimetres of aluminium.

Gamma is very penetrating, needs many centimetres of lead or many metres of concrete to absorb most of it.

HT Radioactive Decay

Ionising radiation is emitted when the nucleus of an unstable atom decays. The type of **radioactive decay** depends on why the nucleus is unstable; the process of decay helps the atom become more **stable**. During decay the number of protons may change. If this happens the element changes to another type.

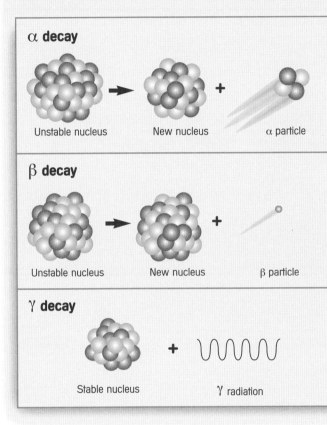

α decay	The original atom decays by ejecting an **alpha** (α) **particle** from the nucleus. This particle is a **helium nucleus**: a particle made of two protons and two neutrons. With **alpha decay** a new atom is formed. This new atom has two protons and two neutrons fewer than the original.
Unstable nucleus · New nucleus · α particle	
β decay	The original atom decays by changing a neutron into a proton and an electron. This high energy electron, which is now ejected from the nucleus, is a **beta** (β) **particle**. With **beta decay** a new atom is formed. This new atom has one more proton and one less neutron than the original.
Unstable nucleus · New nucleus · β particle	
γ decay	After α or β decay, a nucleus sometimes contains surplus energy. It emits this as **gamma** radiation (very high frequency electromagnetic radiation). During gamma decay, only energy is emitted. This decay doesn't change the type of atom.
Stable nucleus · γ radiation	

Background Radiation

Radioactive elements are found naturally in the environment and contribute to **background radiation**. Nothing can stop us being **irradiated** and **contaminated** by background radiation, but generally the levels are so low it's nothing to worry about. However, there's a **correlation** between certain cancers and living in particular areas, especially among people who have lived in granite buildings for many years.

Key Words

Atom • Alpha • Beta • Electron • Element • Gamma • Isotopes • Neutron • Nucleus • Proton

Sources of Background Radiation

Radon gas — Released at surface of ground from uranium in rocks and soil.

From food

Medical — Mainly X-rays.

γ rays — From rocks, soil and building materials.

Cosmic rays — From outer space and the Sun.

Nuclear industry

Radioactive Materials

Half-life

As a radioactive atom decays, its activity drops. This means that its radioactivity decreases over time.

The **half-life** of a substance is the time it takes for its radioactivity to halve.

Different substances have different half-lives, ranging from a few seconds to thousands of years.

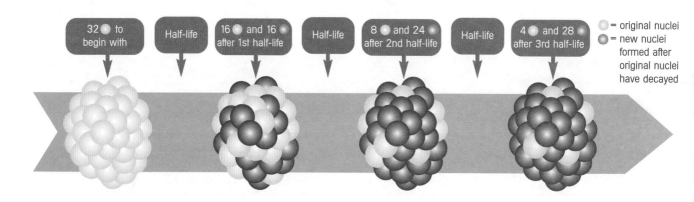

32 ● to begin with

Half-life

16 ● and 16 ● after 1st half-life

Half-life

8 ● and 24 ● after 2nd half-life

Half-life

4 ● and 28 ● after 3rd half-life

● = original nuclei
● = new nuclei formed after original nuclei have decayed

Half-life and Safety

A substance is considered safe once its activity drops to the same level as background radiation. This is a dose of around 2 millisieverts per year or 25 counts per minute with a standard detector.

Some substances decay quickly and could be safe in a very short time. Those with a long half-life remain harmful for thousands of years.

ⓗ Half-life Calculations

The half-life can be used to calculate how old a radioactive substance is, or how long it will take to become safe.

For example, if a sample has an activity of 800 counts per minute and a half-life of 2 hours, how many hours will it take for the activity to reach the background rate of 25 counts per minute?

We need to work out how many half-lives it takes for the sample of 800 counts to reach 25 counts.

① $\dfrac{800}{2}$ = 400
② $\dfrac{400}{2}$ = 200
③ $\dfrac{200}{2}$ = 100
④ $\dfrac{100}{2}$ = 50
⑤ $\dfrac{50}{2}$ = 25

It takes 5 half-lives to reach a count of 25, and each half-life takes 2 hours.

So, it takes 5 x 2 hours = 10 hours.

Dangers of Radiation

Ionising radiation can break molecules into ions. These ions can harm living cells.

HT Ions are **very reactive** and can take part in other chemical reactions.

Many jobs involve using radioactive materials (e.g. the nuclear industry, medical physics). People can become irradiated or **contaminated** so their exposure needs to be carefully monitored.

Different types of radiation carry different risks:

- Alpha is the most dangerous if the source is **inside the body**; all the radiation will be absorbed by cells in the body.
- Beta is the most dangerous if the source is **outside the body**. Unlike alpha, it can penetrate the outer layer of skin and damage internal organs.
- Gamma can cause harm if it's absorbed by the cells, but it is weakly ionising and can pass straight through the body causing no damage at all.

The **sievert** is a measure of a radiation dose's potential to harm a person. It's based on both the type and the amount of radiation absorbed.

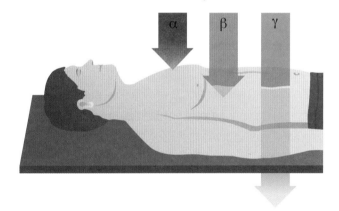

Inside the Body

Outside the Body

Uses of Radiation

Although using ionising radiation can be dangerous, there are many beneficial uses.

High-energy gamma rays in **cancer treatment** can destroy cancer cells but can damage healthy cells too. The radiation has to be carefully targeted from different angles to minimise the damage.

In radiation treatment for cancer there is a danger of damage to healthy cells – doctors need to carefully weigh the risks against the benefits before going ahead.

HT Risks must be assessed and the ALARA principle applied (see page 69).

Radiation is also used to **sterilise surgical instruments** and to **sterilise food**. This kills bacteria.

HT The precautionary principle is applied if the risks are unknown, e.g. only a few foods are allowed radiation treatment and they must carry a label stating this. The priority is to protect the public.

Key Words

ALARA • Alpha • Beta • Gamma • Half-life • Irradiated • Precautionary principle

Radioactive Materials

Electricity

Electricity is a **secondary** energy source. This means it's generated from another energy source, e.g. coal, nuclear power, etc.

Electricity is a very useful energy source as it can be easily transmitted over long distances and used in many ways.

Generating Electricity

To generate electricity, fuel is burned to produce heat:

1. The heat is used to boil water, which produces **steam**.
2. The steam drives the **turbines**, which power the **generators**.
3. Electricity produced in the generators is sent to a **transformer** and then to the National Grid, from where you can access it in your home.

Power stations which burn fossil fuels like coal produce carbon dioxide, a greenhouse gas.

Nuclear power stations release energy due to changes in the **nucleus** of radioactive substances. They don't produce carbon dioxide but they do produce radioactive waste.

Nuclear waste is categorised into three types:

- **High-level waste** (HLW) – very radioactive waste that has to be stored carefully. Fortunately, only small amounts are produced and it doesn't remain radioactive for long, so it's put into short-term storage.
- **Intermediate-level waste** (ILW) – not as radioactive as HLW but it remains radioactive for thousands of years. Increasing amounts are produced; deciding how to store it is a problem. At the moment most ILW is mixed with concrete and stored in big containers, but this isn't a permanent solution.
- **Low-level waste** (LLW) – only slightly radioactive waste that is sealed and placed in landfills.

Electricity from Fossil Fuels

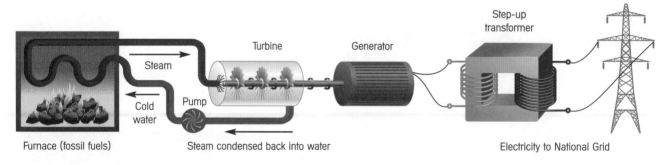

Furnace (fossil fuels) Steam condensed back into water Electricity to National Grid

Electricity from Nuclear Fuels

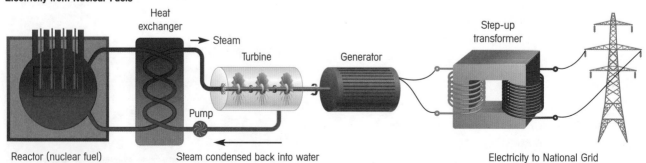

Reactor (nuclear fuel) Steam condensed back into water Electricity to National Grid

Sankey Diagrams

Energy is lost at every stage of the process of electricity generation.

Sankey diagrams can be used to show the generation and distribution of electricity, including the efficiency of energy transfers.

The Sankey diagram shows that from the energy put into the power station, almost half is lost to the surroundings (mostly as heat) before the electricity even reaches the home.

Further energy is lost during energy transfers in the home when the electricity is used.

A Sankey Diagram

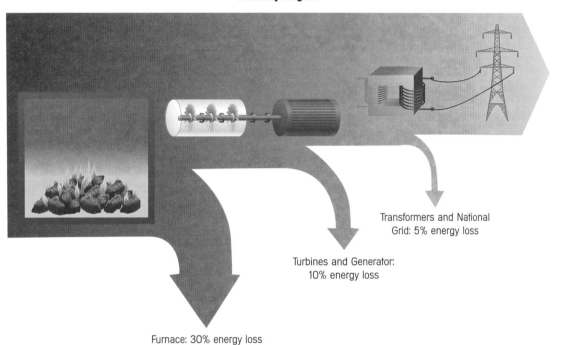

Transformers and National Grid: 5% energy loss

Turbines and Generator: 10% energy loss

Furnace: 30% energy loss

Renewable Energy

Conventional energy supplies are running out and both nuclear and fossil fuels cause environmental damage. This means that **alternative energy sources** are becoming more important.

Alternative ways to generate electricity include **wind**, **water** and **solar** power. These are renewable **energy** sources so will not run out like fossil fuels.

Key Words

Energy transfer • Nuclear waste • Nucleus • Renewable

Radioactive Materials

Wind Turbines

An example of a **renewable energy** source is **wind turbines**. The force of the wind turns the blades of the wind turbine, which provides power to a generator. The amount of electricity produced is small. It would need hundreds of wind turbines to replace a conventional power station. However, once built they provide **free energy**, as long as the wind is blowing.

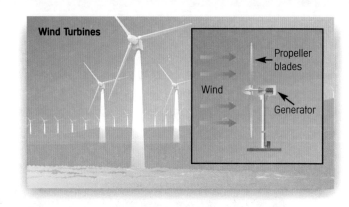

Wind Turbines

Hydroelectric Dam

Hydroelectric dams are another example of a renewable energy source. Water stored in the **reservoir** flows down pipes and turns the turbines, which powers the generators and produces electricity.

Large areas of land may need to be flooded to build **hydroelectric stations**. However, once built they provide large amounts of reliable, fairly cheap energy.

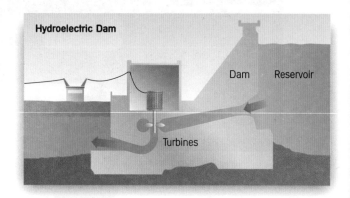

Hydroelectric Dam

Comparing Benefits

When comparing energy sources for generating electricity, the factors used to assess which source is the most favourable are **efficiency**, **cost** and **environmental damage**.

(HT) **Power output** and **lifetime** (how long it lasts for) can also be assessed when comparing energy sources.

Key Words

Chain reaction • Nuclear fission • Nuclear reactor • Uranium

Energy Source	Set-up Cost	Efficiency	Environmental Damage	(HT) Power Output
Nuclear	Very high	Good	• Nuclear radioactive waste	High
Coal	High	Good	• Mining (construction and any waste) • Acid rain • Greenhouse gases • Emissions from the transport of fuel	High
Wind	Low	Variable daily Need a lot of wind	• Visual pollution	Low
Hydroelectric	High	Needs rain	• Changes ecosystem through flooding	High

HT Nuclear Fission

In a **chemical reaction** it is the electrons that cause the change. The elements involved stay the same but join up in different ways.

Nuclear fission takes place in the nucleus of the atom and different elements are formed:

- A **neutron** is absorbed by a large and unstable uranium nucleus. This splits the nucleus into two roughly equal-sized smaller nuclei. This releases energy and more neutrons.
- A fission reaction releases far more energy than even the most **exothermic** chemical reactions. Once fission has taken place the neutrons can be absorbed by other nuclei and further fission reactions can take place. This is a chain reaction.
- A chain reaction occurs when there's enough **fissile material** to prevent too many neutrons escaping without being absorbed. This is called **critical mass** and ensures every reaction triggers at least one further reaction.

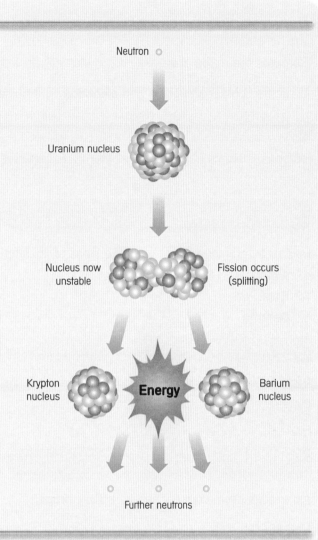

Neutron

Uranium nucleus

Nucleus now unstable — Fission occurs (splitting)

Krypton nucleus — **Energy** — Barium nucleus

Further neutrons

The Nuclear Reactor

Nuclear power stations use fission reactions to generate the heat needed to produce **steam**. The nuclear reactor controls the chain reaction so that the energy is steadily released.

Fission occurs in the **fuel rods** and causes them to become very hot.

The **coolant** is a liquid that is pumped through the reactor. The coolant heats up and is then used in the **heat exchanger** to turn water into steam.

Control rods, made of **boron**, absorb neutrons, preventing the chain reaction getting out of control. Moving the control rods in and out of the **reactor core** changes the amount of fission which takes place.

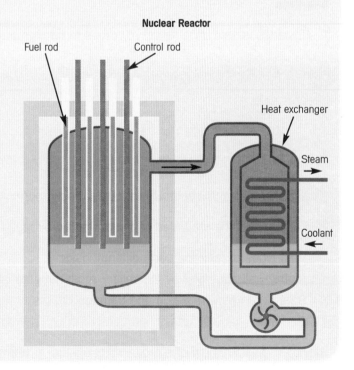

Nuclear Reactor

Fuel rod — Control rod

Heat exchanger

Steam

Coolant

Module P3 Summary

Atoms and Elements

Elements are made of **atoms** – each element contains only one type of atom.

All atoms contain a **nucleus** and **electrons**. The nucleus is made from **protons** and **neutrons**.

(HT) Every atom of a particular element always has the **same number** of protons.

Isotopes = atoms of the **same element** with **different numbers** of neutrons.

Ionising Radiation

Radioactive materials give out three types of ionising radiation:
- **Alpha**.
- **Beta**.
- **Gamma**.

(HT) Ionising radiation is emitted when the nucleus of an **unstable atom decays**.

Radioactive decay helps the atom become more stable. During decay the number of protons may change so the element changes to another type.

Half-Life

As a radioactive atom decays, its activity **drops**.

Half-life = the time it takes for the radioactivity of a substance to halve. **Different substances** have **different half-lives**.

A substance is safe once its activity drops to **background radiation levels**.

(HT) The half-life can be used to calculate how old a radioactive substance is, or how long it will take to become **safe**.

Dangers of Radiation

Radioactive elements contribute to natural background radiation.

People can become **irradiated** or **contaminated** through their job. Their **exposure** needs to be **monitored**.

Different types of radiation carry different risks:
- **Alpha** – all **absorbed** by the cells – most dangerous if the source is inside the body.
- **Beta** – can penetrate skin and **damage** organs.
- **Gamma** – can often pass harmlessly through the body.

Sievert = measurement of a radiation's potential to **harm**.

Module P3 Summary

Uses of Radiation

Ionising radiation is dangerous but has **beneficial uses**:
- Cancer treatment.
- Sterilising surgical instruments.
- Sterilising food.

Electricity

Electricity is a **secondary energy source**.

To produce electricity…
Fuel is burned ➡ Steam drives **turbines** ➡ **Generators** ➡ **Transformer** ➡ **National Grid**.

Power stations produce carbon dioxide, a greenhouse gas.

Nuclear power stations ➡ Release energy from changes in a radioactive substance's nucleus.

Three types of **nuclear waste** are…
- high-level
- intermediate
- Low-level.

Energy is lost at **every stage** of electricity generation. **Sankey diagrams** can show this **energy transfer**.

Renewable Energy

Renewable energy source (e.g. **wind turbines** and **hydroelectric dams**). Will not run out like fossil fuels.

Energy sources are compared for **efficiency; cost; environmental damage**.

(HT) **Power output** and **lifetime** can also be assessed.

Nuclear Fission

Electrons **cause the change** in a chemical reaction; elements stay the same but join up in **different ways**.

Nuclear fission takes place in the **nucleus**:
- A neutron is absorbed by an **unstable** uranium nucleus.
- The nucleus **splits** and releases **energy**.
- A **chain reaction** occurs. **Critical mass**.

Nuclear reactor = controls the chain reaction.

Coolant = heats up and turns water into steam in the **heat exchanger**.

Control rods = made of **boron**, prevent chain reaction getting out of control.

Module P3 Practice Questions

1 a) Name three types of ionising radiation.

i) ....

ii) ....

iii) ....

b) Which type of ionising radiation is the most harmful if it gets into the body?

....

c) Name two beneficial uses of ionising radiation.

i) ....

ii) ....

2 State whether the following statements are true or false. Write your answer in the space provided.

a) The radioactivity of a substance increases over time. ....

b) An atom's activity drops as it decays. ....

c) The half-life of a substance is always less than one thousand years. ....

d) Substances all have the same half-life. ....

e) A substance is safe once its activity drops to background radiation levels. ....

3 Why is electricity described as a secondary energy source?

....

....

4 a) Name two renewable energy sources.

i) ....

ii) ....

b) Name two advantages of renewable energy.

i) ....

ii) ....

5 The diagram shows how electricity is produced from fossil fuels.

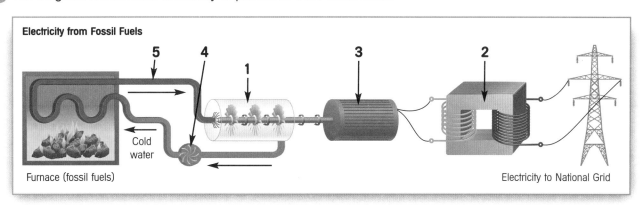

Electricity from Fossil Fuels

5 4 1 3 2

Cold water

Furnace (fossil fuels)

Electricity to National Grid

Match **A, B, C** and **D** with the labels **1–5** on the diagram. Enter the appropriate number in the boxes provided.

A Turbine ◯

B Generator ◯

C Steam ◯

D Pump ◯

E Transformer ◯

HT **6** Fill in the missing words to complete the sentences below:

a) A chain reaction occurs when there's enough _____ material to prevent too

many _____ escaping without being absorbed.

b) The amount of material needed for a chain reaction is called _____ mass.

7 **a)** Where in the nuclear reactor does nuclear fission occur?

_____

b) What is the role of the coolant?

_____

_____

c) What is the role of the control rods?

_____

_____

Glossary of Key Words

Acid rain – rain containing sulfur dioxide and nitrogen oxides.

Additive – a substance added to food to make it last longer or to improve flavour, appearance, etc.

Allele – alternative form of a particular gene.

Allergy – a bad reaction by the body to a substance or food.

Alpha – a radioactive particle made of 2 protons and 2 neutrons.

Amino acid – molecule that is a building block of proteins.

Antibiotic – chemical that kills bacteria and fungi.

Antibody – produced by white blood cells to inactivate disease-causing microorganisms.

Antigen – marker on the surface of a disease-causing microorganism.

Artery – a muscular blood vessel that carries blood away from the heart.

Asexual reproduction – new offspring are reproduced that are identical to the parent.

Atmosphere – the air; the layer of gas surrounding the Earth.

Atom – smallest particle of an element.

Bacteria – a single-celled microorganism that has no nucleus.

Beta – a type of radioactive particle made of an electron.

Big Bang – a theory of how the Universe started.

Biodiversity – range of species in an environment.

Blood sugar – glucose dissolved in the bloodstream.

Carbon cycle – the constant recycling of carbon by the processes in life, death and decay.

Catalytic converter – a device fitted to a car exhaust to reduce the emission of air pollutants.

Central nervous system – the brain and spinal cord, allows an organism to react to its surroundings and coordinates its responses.

Chemical digestion – using chemicals to break down food.

Chemical synthesis – the making of new materials.

Chromosome – a coil of DNA made up of genes, found in the nucleus of plants / animal cells.

Clinical trial – the process of testing a medical treatment or medicine on human volunteers for safety and effectiveness.

Clone – organisms genetically identical to the parent.

Combustion – chemical reaction which occurs when fuels burn, releasing heat.

Common ancestor – the most recent individual from which all organisms in a group are directly descended.

Competition – the demand by two or more organisms for limited environmental resources at the same time.

Compound – substance consisting of two or more elements chemically combined.

Concentration – a measure of the amount of substance dissolved in a solution.

Continental drift – the movement of continents being carried on tectonic plates.

Convection current – carries heat energy in liquids and gases.

Crude oil – a liquid mixture of hydrocarbons found in rocks.

Cystic fibrosis – a hereditary disorder that mainly affects the lungs and digestive system.

Decomposer – an organism that breaks down other matter.

Deforestation – destruction of forests by cutting down trees.

Diabetes – a disease caused by the pancreas not producing and releasing enough insulin.

DNA (deoxyribonucleic acid) – contains the genetic information carried by every cell.

E number – a legal food additive.

Effector – the part of the body, e.g. a muscle or a gland, which produces a response to a stimulus.

Electromagnetic spectrum – a continuous arrangement that displays electromagnetic waves in order of increasing frequency.

Electron – negatively charged particle that orbits the nucleus of an atom.

Element – a substance that consists of one type of atom.

Glossary of Key Words

Energy transfer − the movement of energy from one place to another.

Environmental variation − variation that occurs as a result of a certain factor in the surroundings.

Enzyme − a protein which speeds up a reaction; a biological catalyst.

Epidemiological study − a study of the factors affecting the health and illness of populations.

Erosion − the wearing away of the Earth's surface.

Ethics − the standards by which human actions can be judged right or wrong.

Evolution − the gradual process of adaptation of a species over generations.

Extinct − a species that has died out.

Fertiliser - a substance added to soil to improve the crop yield.

Fetus − an unborn human / animal baby.

Food chain − a simple chain showing the feeding relationship between organisms in an ecosystem.

Food Standards Agency − an independent Government department set up to protect the public's health and consumer interests in relation to food.

Food web − interlinked food chains in an ecosystem.

Fossil − the remains of animals / plants preserved in rock.

Fractional distillation − process used to separate the fractions in crude oil.

Fungi − group of organisms including mushrooms, toadstools and yeasts.

Gamma − a radioactive emission that is an electromagnetic wave.

Gene − a section of a chromosome, made up of DNA.

Gene therapy − the insertion of genes into a patient's cells and tissues to treat a disease or disorder.

Genetic test − a test to determine if an individual has a genetic disorder.

Geohazard − any natural hazard associated with the Earth, e.g. earthquake.

Global warming − an Increase In the temperature of the Earth, caused by an increase in greenhouse gases.

Gravity − a force of attraction between all masses.

Greenhouse effect − the process that keeps the Earth warm by reflecting heat back to Earth.

Greenhouse gas − gas in the Earth's atmosphere that absorbs radiation and stops it from leaving the Earth's atmosphere.

Half-life − the time taken for the radioactivity of a substance to halve.

Hominid − any member of the biological family Hominidae (the "great apes").

Hormone − a regulatory substance which stimulates cells or tissues into action.

Huntington's disorder − a hereditary, degenerative disorder of the central nervous system.

Hydrocarbon − compound made of carbon and hydrogen atoms only.

Immune system − the body's defence system against infections and diseases (consists of white blood cells and antibodies).

Incineration − disposing of something by burning it.

Insulin − a hormone, produced by the pancreas, which controls blood glucose concentrations.

Intensive farming − method of farming that uses fertilisers, pesticides and controlled environments to maximise food production.

***In vitro* fertilisation** (IVF) − a technique in which egg cells are fertilised outside the female body.

Ion − charged particle formed when an atom gains or loses an electron.

Irradiated − to be exposed to radioactive emissions.

Landfill − disposing of rubbish in holes in the ground.

Life Cycle Assessment − an assessment of a product from manufacture to disposal.

Light speed − the speed light travels at.

Light year − the distance light travels in one year.

Monomer − a small hydrocarbon molecule.

Mutation − a spontaneous change in the genetic code of a cell.

Natural immunity − to remain resistant to or be unaffected by a specific disease.

Natural selection − a natural process resulting in the evolution of organisms best adapted to the environment.

Glossary of Key Words

Neurone – specialised cell which transmits electrical messages or nerve impulses.

Neutron – particle in the nucleus of an atom that has no charge.

Neutron star – the extremely dense remainder of some of the largest stars.

Nitrogen Cycle – the recycling of nitrogen and its compounds in nature.

Non-biodegradable – a substance that does not decompose naturally by the action of microorganisms.

Nuclear fusion – the joining of atomic nuclei.

Nuclear waste – the radioactive waste left over as a byproduct of nuclear power generation.

Nucleus – control centre of a cell.

Organic farming – farming that uses natural fertilisers and natural methods of controlling pests with an emphasis on quality rather than quantity.

Outlier – a value outside the usual range of values.

Ozone layer – the layer of gas in the upper atmosphere that absorbs ultraviolet radiation.

Pancreas – organ in the body that produces insulin.

Peer review – the process by which new scientific ideas and discoveries are validated by other scientists.

Pesticide – a chemical used to destroy insects or other pests.

Photon – a 'packet' of energy carried by electromagnetic radiation.

Photosynthesis – process by which plants make food using light energy from the Sun.

Physical digestion – chewing and squeezing food to break it down inside the body.

Plasticizer – a material added to a plastic to make it more bendy.

Pollutant – a chemical that can harm the environment and health.

Polymer – a giant long-chained hydrocarbon.

Polymerisation – the joining of monomers to make a polymer.

Product – substance made in a chemical reaction.

Protein – large organic compounds made of amino acids.

Proton – particle in the nucleus of an atom that has a positive charge.

Radiation – electromagnetic waves / particles emitted by a radioactive substance.

Reactant – substance at the start of a chemical reaction.

Recycling – re-using materials that would otherwise be considered waste.

Renewable – source which will not run out.

Risk – the danger (normally to health) associated with a procedure, action or event.

Scientific advisory committee – committee of independent experts who advise on scientific issues.

Selective breeding – the production of new varieties of animals and plants by artificial selection.

Sensor – detects a stimulus.

Side effect – condition caused by taking medication, e.g. headache, nausea.

Stem cell – a cell from an embryo or adult bone marrow which has yet to differentiate.

Stimulus – a change in an organism's environment.

Supernova – an exploding star.

Survival of the fittest – process by which the organisms that are best adapted to their environment survive to pass on their successful traits to their offspring.

Sustainable – capable of being continued with minimal long-term effect on the environment.

Tectonic plate – huge sections of the Earth's crust which move in relation to one another.

Theory of Evolution – the most likely scientific explanation, based on evidence, as to why organisms are the way they are.

Variable – a value that can change.

Variation – differences between individuals of the same species.

Vein – a blood vessel that carries blood towards the heart.

Virus – tiny microorganism with a very simple structure that is reliant on using a cell's machinery to reproduce.

HT ALARA – As Low As Reasonably Achievable; a policy of minimising risk while still providing the benefits.

Chain reaction – when a nuclear fission reaction becomes self-sustaining.

Crystalline – a solid formed by a regular, repeating 3-D arrangement of particles.

Hubble's Law – states that the further away a galaxy is, the faster it is moving away from us.

Isotopes – atoms of the same element which contain different numbers of neutrons.

Magnetic field – the lines of force surrounding a magnet or the Earth.

Nuclear fission – the splitting of atomic nuclei.

Nuclear reactor – the place where fission takes place in a nuclear power station.

Precautionary principle – experts and the public are consulted if scientific evidence is uncertain and the risks are unknown; the costs and benefits are then weighed up.

Placebo – dummy medical treatment that is inert (does not work), such as a sugar pill.

Pre-implantation Genetic Diagnosis – involves removing a cell from an embryo at an early stage of development and testing it for genetic disorders.

Sex-determining region Y – a sex-determining gene on the Y chromosome in humans and other primates.

Subduction – when an oceanic plate is forced under a continental plate.

Uranium – a radioactive element often used as nuclear fuel.

Answers to Practice Questions

Module B1

1. A gene provides instructions to make **proteins**.
2. **a)–b) In any order:** Structural proteins; Enzymes.
3. Different versions of the same gene are called **alleles**.
4.

    Offspring **BB**   **Bb**   **Bb**   **bb**

               Brown   Brown   Brown   Blue

5. **a)** chromosomes   **b)** asexual   **c)** clones
    d) environmental   **e)** sexual   **f)** X
6. **a)** The central nervous system.
    b) **i)** Continuous, involuntary movement; Dementia.
        ii) Any two from: Weight loss; Troublesome coughs; Repeated
        chest infections; Salty sweat; Abnormal faeces.
7. Amniocentesis testing and Chorionic Villus testing.

8. True Positive – Fetus **has** the disorder – Fetus **has** the disorder.
    True Negative – Fetus **does not** have the disorder – Fetus **does
    not** have the disorder.
    False Positive – Fetus **has** the disorder – Fetus **does not** have
    the disorder.
    False Negative – Fetus **does not** have the disorder – Fetus **has**
    the disorder.
9. Bacteria and other **single-cell** organisms can **reproduce** by
    dividing to form two new individuals.
10.

    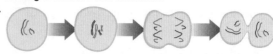

    Cell divides for   Each cell is
    the only time.   identical to the
                         parental cell.

Module C1

1. **a)** The main gas in the atmosphere is **nitrogen**.
    b) 21% of the atmosphere is made up of **oxygen**.
2. A measurement that stands out as being very different to the rest
    of the collected data.
3. **a)** To get a better measurement of the concentration.
    b) 220
    c) Mean = $\dfrac{\text{Sum of values}}{\text{Number of values}}$
    d) 355ppm
4. C and D.
5.

Carbon dioxide	+	Water
$CO_2(g)$	+	$2H_2O(l)$

    O C O   +   H O H / H O H

6. 200
7. Carbon dioxide gas is produced by burning **fuels**. Plants use some
    for **photosynthesis**, some **dissolves** in rain and sea water and
    some stays in the air, increasing the **concentration**.
8. **a)** Carbon.
    b) The sulfur is released as sulfur dioxide.
    c) Acid rain.
9. Oxidation.
10. **a)–b) In any order:** Burn a different type of coal (containing less
    sulfur); Filter the emissions before release.
11. A, B, E, G, H.

Module P1

1. A2, B3, C4, D1.
2. A, C, E.
3. **a)** Earth's crust is divided into **tectonic** plates.
    b) **i)–iii) In any order:** Plates slide past each other; Plates move
        away from each other; Plates move towards each other.
4. **a)** **Convection** currents in the **mantle** cause **magma** to rise and
        form new oceanic crust.
    b) Seafloor spreading.
5. 5000 million years old.
6. **a)** The Solar System began when **dust** and **gas** clouds were
        pulled together by **gravity** which created intense **heat**.
    b) **Nuclear** fusion began and the Sun was born.
    c) Smaller masses also formed, which **orbit** the Sun.

7. **a)–b) In any order:** Planets; Asteroids; Comets; Moons.
8. Light years.
9. **a)–b) In any order:** Relative brightness; Parallax.
10. **a)** The red giant's core contracts and it becomes a planetary
        nebula.
    b) The star's core cools and contracts further, becoming a **white**
        dwarf.
    c) It cools further to become a **black** dwarf.
11. If a source of light is moving away from us, the **wavelengths** of
    light are **longer** than if the source was stationary.
12. The Big Bang theory.

Answers to Practice Questions

Module B2

1. **a)–c) In any order:** Bacteria; Fungi; Viruses.
2. Warmth; Food; Humidity.
3. **a)** Tears.
   b) Stomach acid.
   c) Skin.
   d) Sweat.
4. B, D, A, C.
5. **a)** White blood cell.
   b) Antibody.
   c) Antigen.
   d) Microorganism.

6. B.
7. **a)** There is a small chance of side effects occurring.
   b) The virus causing the disease mutates, producing a new strain that's unaffected by the current vaccine.
8. A, C, D.
9. To make sure that all the bacteria are killed and none survive to become immune to the antibiotic.
10. The main blood vessels are **arteries** and **veins**. Heart attacks occur when **fatty** deposits build up in **vessels** supplying the heart.
11. A4, B3, C1, D6, E2, F5.

Module C2

1. **a)–b) Any two from:** Silk; Wool; Cotton.
2. **a)** Natural materials are extracted from **plants** and **animals** whereas synthetic materials are manufactured from simple **chemicals**.
   b) Crude oil is mainly made up of **hydrocarbons**.
   c) A small proportion of crude oil is used in chemical **synthesis**.
3. A, E and F.
4. **a)–b) In any order:** Lightweight; Water resistant.
5. **a)** During polymerisation, small **hydrocarbon** molecules called **monomers** join together to make very long molecules.
   b)

6. Crosslinks are formed by atoms bonding between polymer molecules so they can no longer move.
7. B.
8. A plasticizer is a small molecule that sits in between the polymer molecules. It makes the polymer more flexible.
9. **a)** **i)** Manufacture.
      ii) Use.
      iii) Disposal.
   b) Each part of the life cycle is assessed for its **environmental** impact and the amount of **materials** and **energy** used.
   c) Attractiveness.
10. **a)–c) In any order:** Landfill; Incineration; Recycling.

Module P2

1. **a)** A **beam** of electromagnetic radiation contains **packets** of energy called **photons**.
   b) Radiation energy travels from a source known as an **emitter** to a **detector**.
2. **a)** Intensity depends on the number of **photons** delivered per **second** and the amount of **energy** each **packet** contains.
   b) A.
   c) **i)–iii) In any order:** Photons spread out; Photons are reflected; Photons are absorbed.
3. **a)–b) Any two from:** Ultraviolet rays; X-rays; Gamma rays.
4. **a)–b) Any two from:** Sunburn; Ageing of the skin; Mutations in the cell which can lead to cancer; Radiation poisoning.
5. **a)** The ozone layer.
   b) It absorbs ultraviolet radiation before it reaches Earth.

   c) Harmful amounts of radiation would get through and living organisms would suffer cell damage.
   d) Ultraviolet radiation causes **reversible** chemical changes in the upper atmosphere.
6. **a)** Carbon dioxide levels stayed constant because animals and plants recycled it.
   b) **i)–ii) In any order:** Burning fossil fuels; Deforestation.
7. **a)–c) In any order: Climate change:** Crops may not grow in some areas; **Extreme weather:** Hurricanes; Drought; **Rising sea levels:** Melting ice caps; Sea levels rising; Low-lying land flooding.
8. **a)** As Low As Reasonably Achievable.
   b) Measures should be taken to make the risks as small as possible, whilst still providing the benefits and taking into account social, economic and practical implications.

Answers to Practice Questions

Module B3

1. 3500 million years ago.
2. **a)–b) In any order:** Cellular structure is similar; Genetic code is similar.
3. **a)** Fossils show the **history** of species and the **evolutionary** changes over millions of years.
   b) Analysing **DNA** can be used to fill gaps in the fossil record.
   c) The more shared **genes** organisms have, the more closely **related** they are.
4. A, C, D E.
5. Environmental variation is when a characteristic is caused by the environment rather than by genetics, so the characteristic can't be passed on. **Accept any suitable example.**

6. Selective breeding is when animals and plants with certain traits are deliberately **mated** to provide offspring with desirable **characteristics**.
7. **a)–b) Any three from:** Increased competition; New predators; Changes to the environment; New diseases; Human activities e.g industry, deforestation.
8. Biodiversity is important because without **variety** we would run out of food, medicines and **resources**.
9.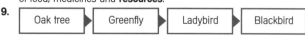

   | Oak tree ▸ | Greenfly ▸ | Ladybird ▸ | Blackbird |

10. **a)–b) In any order:** Hormones; Nerves.
11. A2, B5, C1, D3, E4.

Module C3

1. When plants take in nitrogen they use it to make **amino** acids and **proteins**.
2. A, B, C, F.
3. **a)** Intensive farming uses fertilisers and pesticides, whereas organic farming uses natural methods.
   b) **i) Any one from:** Food costs less; Higher yields; Less labour intensive.
   ii) Any one from: Sustainable; Less environmental damage; More local employment.
4. **a)–c) Any three from:** Additives can make food taste better; To make it more visually appealing; To extend the shelf life; To make the product sweeter without using sugar.
5. **a)–b) Any two from:** Keep the kitchen clean; Dispose of waste quickly; Cook food properly; Store food correctly; Buy organic food to avoid pesticides.

6. The FSA will ask a **scientific** advisory committee to decide if an additive should be used and carry out a **risk** assessment.
7. True.
8. **a)** **Starch** is broken down into **glucose** during digestion so that it's small enough to pass through the **intestine** wall and be absorbed into the **bloodstream**.
   b) Hair, muscle and haemoglobin consist mainly of **protein**.
9. **a)** They are broken down to form urea.
   b) Liver.
10. A balanced diet helps you stay healthy so can reduce the chances of diseases like obesity and heart disease.
11. People with diabetes cannot control blood sugar levels, which can lead to problems.
12. Insulin is produced in the **pancreas**.
13. A, B, C, D and F.

Module P3

1. **a)** **i)–iii) In any order:** Alpha; Beta; Gamma.
   b) Alpha.
   c) **i)–ii) Any two from:** Cancer treatment; Sterilising surgical instruments; Sterilising food.
2. **a)** False.
   b) True.
   c) False.
   d) False.
   e) True.
3. Electricity is generated from another energy source such as fossil fuels or nuclear power.
4. **a)** **i)–ii) Any two from:** Wind power, Hydroelectric power; Solar power.
   b) **i)–ii) Any two from:** Kinder to the environment; Cheaper; Will not run out like fossil fuels.

5. A1, B3, C5, D4, E2.
6. **a)** A chain reaction occurs when there's enough **fissile** material to prevent too many **neutrons** escaping without being absorbed.
   b) The amount of material needed for a chain reaction is called **critical** mass.
7. **a)** Fuel rods.
   b) It transfers heat energy from the reactor to the heat exchanger, where it heats water and turns it into steam.
   c) Control rods prevent the chain reaction getting out of control.

Notes